"The Linotype
is the
Eighth Wonder
of the
World."

–attributed to
Thomas Alva Edison

Above:
The "Blower" Linotype of 1886, first model used commercially.

Right:
Mergenthaler's redesigned (1889) Linotype, star base Model 1 — the master pattern for all the machines produced from 1890 on.

THE BIOGRAPHY OF
Ottmar
Mergenthaler

INVENTOR OF THE LINOTYPE

◆

A New Edition,
With Added Historical Notes
Based On Recent Findings

◆

Researched and Edited by
CARL SCHLESINGER

◆

INTRODUCTION BY ELIZABETH HARRIS

OAK KNOLL SERIES
ON
THE HISTORY OF THE BOOK

Copyright 1989 by Carl Schlesinger

All rights reserved. No form of reproduction of any part of this book shall be made without written permission of the copyright holder, except for brief quotations embodied in critical articles and reviews. For more information please address the Copyright Holder c/o the Publisher.

PUBLISHED BY OAK KNOLL BOOKS
414 Delaware Street • New Castle, Delaware 19720

Library of Congress Cataloging in Publication Data

Mergenthaler, Ottmar, 1854-1899.
    Autobiography of Ottmar Mergenthaler, inventor of the linotype.
    (Oak Knoll series on the history of the book)
    Originally published: Biography of Ottmar Mergenthaler and history of the linotype. Baltimore. 1898.
    Bibliography: p. 122.
    Includes index.
    1. Linotype. 2. Mergenthaler, Ottmar, 1854-1899. 3. Inventors—United States—Biography. 4. Type-setting Machines—History. I. Schlesinger, Carl. II. Title. III. Series.
Z253.M48   1988   686.2'24'0924 [B] 88-92646
ISBN 0-938768-12-3
ISBN 0-938768-13-1 (Special ed.)

ALSO BY CARL SCHLESINGER

Union Printers and Controlled Automation (Craftsmen's Reactions to Linotype & Computers) Co-authored with Prof. Harry Kelber (New York: Free Press, 1967).

Farewell etaoin shrdlu (Last night of hot-metal typesetting at The New York Times—Documentary movie) Created with Producer-Director David Loeb Weiss, 1978 (Circulating Film Library, Museum of Modern Art, New York City 10019).

Contents

List of Illustrations, Diagrams, Tables vi
FOREWORD
    Dr. Wolfgang Kummer, Linotype AG vii
INTRODUCTION
    Elizabeth Harris, National Museum of American History ix
ACKNOWLEDGMENTS
    Carl Schlesinger, Editor xiii

PART I

AN EXPLANATION OF MERGENTHALER'S "BIOGRAPHY":
    Stephen O. Saxe, APHA Newsletter xvi
THE BIOGRAPHY OF OTTMAR MERGENTHALER 1
INDEX 75
MERGENTHALER'S BALTIMORE CATALOG 76

PART II

"THE LINOTYPE—REVOLUTION IN PRINTING"
    May 19, 1889 *New York Tribune* Story 87
HISTORIC PHOTOGRAPHS
    New York Tribune building; first Linotype operator,
    Mergenthaler seen by three artists 95

PART III

DISCOVERY OF MERGENTHALER'S SECRET MATRICES
    and THE HIDDEN *TRIBUNE* LINOTYPE STORIES 101
THE FIRST BOOK SET ON A LINOTYPE 120
BIBLIOGRAPHY 122
INDEX 123
"THE GENIUS OF THE WORKSHOP"
    Editorial from Editor & Publisher 124
NEWSPAPER PAGE WITH FIRST LINOTYPE STORIES . . . . Inside Back Cover

Illustrations, Diagrams and Tables

The "Blower" Linotype 1886 ii
Model 1 Linotype, 1890 ii
Otto Schoenrich's Dedication, Mergenthaler Biography xvii
Ottmar Mergenthaler, 1894 xviii
Ottmar Mergenthaler, 1879 2
James O. Clephane 6
Rotary impression machine, 1879 9
L. G. Hine 12
First band machine, 1883 14
Direct casting band machine, 1884 16
First machine with circulating matrices, 1885 23
New York Tribune "Blower" machine, 1886 27
Model 1 Linotype, 1890 57
Mergenthaler 1898 Baltimore factory catalog, front cover 77
View of Baltimore factory 79
Steel matrix department, Baltimore factory 80
Steel matrix illustration 81
Experimenting room, Baltimore factory 82
Front office, Baltimore factory 84
First Linotype slugs, 1885, galley proof 86
New York Tribune building 95
First Linotype operator 96
New York Public Library Mergenthaler mural 98
Mergenthaler and Reid (Coggeshall Wilson drawing) 99
Mergenthaler and Reid (John DePol engraving) 100
Tribune miniature editorial page, 1886 102
Punchcutter Harry Carter at work 108
Making matrices, casting hand type, drawing 109
Matrix samples, casting Linotype slugs, drawing 110
Theory of electrotyping of matrices, drawing 111
Letter and telegram about electrotyped matrices 112
Phantom diagram of Linotype circulating matrices 118
Table of point sizes 119
Tribune Book of Open-Air Sports, photo of book 120
Tribune Book of Open-Air Sports, typical page 121

Foreword

*"We are going to have full success
for the reason that we have attacked
the problem in an entirely different way
than did those who have failed."*

Ottmar Mergenthaler, 1885

THOMAS EDISON described the Linotype machine as "the Eighth Wonder of the World" because it solved the problem of how to set type without using individual pieces. The device, the greatest advance in typesetting in the 400 years since Gutenberg, revolutionized the craft of printing.

The success of the Linotype can perhaps be attributed to the persistence as well as the perspicacity of its inventor. As a young man, Mergenthaler was impressed by the slow, laborious methods used for type composition. He began to work on various designs for type composition machines that would improve the process, doing both the conceptual work and the actual drawings.

Over a period of years, he developed several machines, but none solved the problem to his satisfaction. The solution came as so many of the great breakthroughs do: as pure inspiration. While on a train bound for Washington, D.C., Mergenthaler realized that the answer was to combine the casting and composition processes into one machine.

He enthusiastically pursued this course and on July 3, 1886, he showed the new machine to Whitelaw Reid, his chief financial backer. As he picked up a hot slug from the machine, Reid exclaimed, "Ottmar, you've done it! You've cast a line of type!" The description fitted so aptly that Mergenthaler's breakthrough soon became known as the Linotype machine.

Quickly adopted by major newspapers the world over, the Linotype machine ushered in an era of high-speed, low-cost and high-quality composition of every kind. Soon afterwards more and more typefaces were made available for the Linotype system. These designs were made not only for the English and European left-to-right-reading languages but also for reading systems that read right to left. The well-engineered Linotype was easily adapted to accommodate these languages. The result was a new degree of freedom worldwide in the creation of everything from newspapers to books of every kind, from advertisements to a wide range of literature that suited the needs of modern and growing businesses.

For his creation of the Linotype, Ottmar Mergenthaler has been justly recognized as one of the 19th century's great inventors. Yet few people realize just what an impact this one man had. Today thousands of devices, in many fields of endeavor, use ideas that descended from Mergenthaler's original Linotype machine.

Since Mergenthaler's Linotype we have progressed through several generations of typesetting technology. We have evolved gradually through phototypesetting, digital typesetting and have arrived at today's laser image-setting. All these sophisticated technologies, however, owe much to the solid foundation provided by Ottmar Mergenthaler in 1886. It is fitting that, as the printing industry continues to undergo dramatic technological change, the life story of a man who revolutionized it is being re-issued.

DR. WOLFGANG KUMMER
Chairman of the Executive Board
Linotype AG

September 1, 1988

Introduction

OTTMAR MERGENTHALER was born in 1854, the son of a schoolteacher in Hachtel, a small town in southern Germany. The young Ottmar had a talent for mechanical tinkering which was recognized and encouraged by his family, in particular his uncle Louis Hahl, a watchmaker. At the age of fourteen Ottmar was taken on as an apprentice in his uncle's shop, and at seventeen, a freshly trained journeyman, he set out to find a new life in America. Hahl's son August had already established himself as a watchmaker and model builder in Washington D.C.; Ottmar joined his cousin there in 1872 and a few years later moved with Hahl and his shop to Baltimore. At this time the Patent Office required that every patentee provide a scale model in support of an application for a patent. Clearly there was business for clever modelmakers.

Among the customers at Hahl's Baltimore office was Charles Moore, the inventor of a typewriting system, whose inquiries were to steer Mergenthaler towards the invention of the Linotype. Mechanical type writing and type setting were not new ideas. They had attracted able minds in Europe and America for two generations and by 1874, when Moore and Clephane put in their appearance, several typesetting machines were in regular use in large printing offices. But Moore and his financial partner James Clephane were working on the invention of a system that would make a direct link between the office desk and the printing press, bypassing both typefounder and compositor.

Almost all 19th century typesetting systems began with a keyboard borrowed from the typewriter. Most shared the aim of mechanizing the ordinary tasks of the printing office: the composition of precast letters, the justification of lines, and the redistribution of the letters after printing. Newspapers used up huge quantities of type, so some systems designed specifically for newspaper work dispensed with distribution and included a typecasting unit instead, providing fresh type for every issue of the paper. Other machines used and reused nick-coded type specially cast for the purpose.

William Church of Vermont and later Birmingham, England, devised the first true composing machine in 1822 and paired it with a typecaster. His machines may never have become a practical reality, but they lived on in legend as the ancestors of the tribe. The first commercially successful composer machine in the world was the Anglo-French "Pianotyp" of James Young and Adrien Delcambre, patented in London and the U.S. (1840-41) and used in several periodical printing offices in London in the 1840s. This machine had separate setting and distributing units, and employed an extra boy to justify the lines of type.

The first truly home-grown American typesetting machine was patented by William Hazlet Mitchel of Brooklyn in 1850, and used in the large New York printing shop of John F. Trow. As with the Pianotyp, Mitchel's system provided separate setting and (in 1854) distributing machines with justification by hand. Mitchel was followed in 1857 by Timothy Alden of Yarmouth, Massachusetts, who built a composer and distributor into the same machine. Alden's machines were used in the New York *Herald* in 1857; the Alden Typesetting Machine Company survived at least until 1910.[1]

The "Burr" (later "Empire") composer and distributor of 1872 were the first American machines to be used on both sides of the Atlantic. In the same year Alexander Fraser of Edinburgh patented composing and distributing machines in both countries; Fraser's machines were to set 10,000 pages of the *Encyclopedia Britannica* in 1888. In 1880 Joseph Thorne, a New Englander, combined composition and distribution into a single machine which was operated by one man, and was later renamed the Unitype or "Simplex one-man typesetter" in honor of this fact. Justification was still separate and by hand; it was proving the hardest of the problems to solve.

The machine that James Moore presented to Mergenthaler in 1876 was a typewriter that produced a continuous strip of copy ready for immediate transfer to a lithographic stone—avoiding the troublesome matters of justification and distribution. But after overcoming major technical challenges to produce clear even print, the inventors were beaten by apparently lesser problems at the lithographic stage, perhaps because of their lack of experience with the process. Mergenthaler persuaded Moore and Clephane to change to a machine to impress letters or whole words into papier mache for stereotype casting.

Four years later he convinced them to replace the rotary matrix machine with a machine that indented papier mache matrices from continuous metal bands of letter patrices. Then in rapid succession he produced the second band machine which made a slug of type from letter matrices, an improved version with automatic justification (1884), the single matrix machine ("Blower") which produced a slug of type from separate and circulating matrices (1886), and the Square-base Linotype in 1888.

This pattern of development, and the philosophy underlying it, might be acceptable in the industry today, but Mergenthaler's backers of the 1880s had set their hopes and money on seeing one ultimate and perfect machine. They showed increasing nervousness with each proposed improvement. As Hine remarked, "not many shareholders can stand being told that we have the best machine in the world, but that we are going to make another which is still better." In 1887 and again in 1890 Mergenthaler was forbidden to make any further changes to the machine.

The most serious competition for the Linotype machine in Mergenthaler's lifetime came from the John Rogers' "Typograph," a smaller linecaster which was, as Mergenthaler states, barred by court injunction from production in the United States (it continued to be made and sold in Canada and Europe). The dealings were more involved than Mergenthaler admits[2]. Rogers had acquired the rights to a double-wedge space band invented and patented by J. W. Shuckers, beating Mergenthaler for the patent rights to a similar device by a few months. Mergenthaler's company eventually obtained the space band by buying out the Rogers company.

With the change from the patrix to the matrix machine, Mergenthaler broke into the domain of the typefounding trade and encountered opposition that he seems never to have understood. American type founders had seen their business expand from a very limited trade in the 1830s, centered in a few major cities and still contending with competition from European shops, to a large and flourishing industry with a representative, or several, in every large town. Thanks to the electrotyping process developed in the 1850s piracy of type faces was easy and rife, so a given face could be had from many sources. But a customer was likely to be tied to his first supplier for all later orders because the founders used the devious ploy of casting type on nonstandard bodies; thus, type from Foundry X would only work with other type from that foundry. Typefounders rode on the backs of the newspapers, increasing in number with them, for the type demands of a daily paper were enough to support a foundry.

This situation pleased the founders better than the newspapermen. It was not by chance that the invention of the Linotype was opposed by typefounders and supported by a syndicate of newspaper publishers, or that the first 200 production models were installed in newspaper offices. One can even believe that Mergenthaler was right in one of his complaints against the "baleful work of the syndicate"—that in 1888, having supplied themselves with Linotype machines, the publishers tried to discredit the machine publicly and thus limit it to their own circle. In that, they certainly failed. The Linotype was adopted by many other newspaper offices within a few years. As a direct result, in 1892 twenty-three independent American typefoundries were forced into a defensive amalgamation, the American Typefounders Company. The American typefounding industry never regained its strength.

For Ottmar Mergenthaler, the story did not end happily. The misunderstandings between the businessmen and the brilliant and impulsive inventor grew to become overwhelming. This book, Mergenthaler's anonymous account of his invention and his trials, was printed in 1898. Mergenthaler died of tuberculosis in Baltimore the following year, still young and an embittered man[3]. Philip Dodge, the man who in 1891 took over the presidency of the company and along with it Mergenthaler's enmity, remained in that office until his retirement in 1928.

> ELIZABETH HARRIS
> Curator, Division of Graphic Arts,
> National Museum of American History
> Smithsonian Institution

September 6, 1988

NOTES

1. Huss, Richard E.: *The development of printer's mechanical typesetting methods 1822-1925* (University Press of Virginia, 1973) p 49; and Legros, Lucien A. and John C. Grant, *Typographical printing surfaces* (London 1916) p 655.
2. Huss, Richard E., op. cit. p 133.
3. The most thorough account of Mergenthaler's life, inventions and circumstances is in George Corban Goble's dissertation, "The obituary of a machine: the rise and fall of Ottmar Mergenthaler's Linotype at U.S. newspapers" (Indiana University, 1984).

Comments and Acknowledgments

THROUGH publication of this book I hope to add more substance to what is known of events in the life of one of the world's great inventors. We start with Stephen Saxe's proof that the uncredited book *Biography of Ottmar Mergenthaler* is actually the inventor's own thoughts and opinions. These were written down for him in 1898 by his associate Otto Schoenrich. Following that section is the first-time reprinting of an important newspaper article of 1889, which describes the effects of the installation of the first Linotype. Inventing the machine was Mergenthaler's most important life accomplishment.

The final inclusion is my research on the inventor's development of electrotyped matrices, which he used to cast his first live types—an event never before reported.

Since all the above still does not add up to a fully rounded story, the reader is urged to consult the Bibliography at the back of this book. Further interest on some reader's part may bring out more discoveries. Each piece of new knowledge will help us learn more about Mergenthaler's regrettably short life, which ended at only 45, well before reaching the peak of his powers.

Mergenthaler's invention of the Linotype changed forever the way that type was composed, and it considerably increased the speed at which composition was done. In the early 1890's, as the Linotype company was leasing and selling the new typesetting machine in printing shops throughout America, its installation helped bring about the near-bankruptcy and consolidation of twenty-three hand-type foundries. Some 12,000 composing room workers were estimated to have been displaced and/or became unemployed during the period 1890 to 1910. It is clear that in the short run an invention like this, which severely affected the industry, could not mean good news to employed hand compositors.

Within the space of that same twenty years, however, a metamorphosis of the typesetting industry also occurred. America's economy had faltered in the early 1890s, but it gained strength again as it entered the 20th century. Typesetters got their share of that prosperity. By 1910 more jobs, including thousands of positions for new and retrained Linotype operators, had been created. The Linotype's speedy diffusion of printed knowledge at low cost made possible more textbooks for schools, more books and magazines for libraries and bookstores and bigger, more comprehensive newspapers. With the easier availability of Linotype-printed materials in many languages, literacy increased throughout the world.

Millionaire Andrew Carnegie was a steelworks employer who became a respected philanthropist in his later years. One of his gifts in the early 1900's was the creation of 2800 free libraries in towns across America. While Carnegie's structures of stone, steel and wood were being built, Mergenthaler's Linotype was busy helping to fill these buildings with newly printed books. Let the following situation demonstrate the Linotype's great impact on mid-20th century printing.

In the 1880's almost all books in America were composed by using hand-set type. By 1961, only seventy-five years after the Linotype's invention, a major change had taken place. More than eighty percent of all the books on the shelves of America's libraries had by then been composed, and were being composed, using the Linotype machine.

The change in typesetting methods was even more pronounced in the magazine and newspaper field. Practically every magazine and newspaper in America in the 1880's was set by hand. By 1961, however, the reverse had taken place: Linotypes were being used to compose the text matter for almost every magazine and daily and weekly newspaper. This was quite an impact for an invention to have on America's main communications media.

There is still another facet to examine. The Linotype's ability to automatically redistribute and re-use its circulating matrices meant that owners of the machines were guaranteed a never-ending supply of new type, at very low cost. As far as actual physical work was concerned, there was an even greater benefit. No longer would compositors have to painstakingly return thousands of pieces of used type to their storage cases each day so that there would be a supply for the next day's setting. In newspapers, printers spent more than two hours each day doing this non-productive redistribution work. That task was now cheerfully taken over by the Linotype machine's recirculating matrices.

But who would gain the two hours a day that each printer saved? During the 1890's and early 1900's the Typographical Union patiently negotiated with employers for the saved time, firmly pointing out that the benefits of increased machine productivity should be shared with the workforce. Through new contract agreements the printer's workday gradually was lowered from ten and twelve hours to eight and even seven hours a day, six days a week. Production did not suffer unduly as machines continued to be built more efficiently and operators became more skilled. This betterment of working conditions was another plus, brought on by Mergenthaler's ingenious, time-saving invention.

Mergenthaler's desire to improve his machine continued even after the company's officers forbade him to make any more changes. It reminds me of a rhymed saying my daughters learned at school that goes: "Good, better, best/ Never let it rest/'Till your 'good' is 'better'/And your 'better' is 'best'."

Only a driven person could try to live up to that ambitious advice—and only an inspired inventor like Mergenthaler could come close to succeeding before paying his final tragic price.

Like a plant coming to flower, this book took a long time to grow. I'd like to thank those who gave me regular intellectual nourishment, so that more than two years of work could finally be channelled between these covers. First mention goes to Dr. Corban Goble, whose great dissertation started me down my own research path; next comes Richard Hopkins, founder of the American Typecasting Fellowship, whose encouragement helped me make my decision to produce the work. Stephen Saxe not only gave encouragement but also kindly lent his original Mergenthaler *Biography* copy and his Baltimore catalog; both are reproduced in these pages. Elizabeth Harris honored me with sound advice as well as her comprehensive Introduction.

Stan Nelson and Theo Rehak reviewed my copy and helped with technical information while Prof. Terry Belanger, Irving Lipner and Leonard Harris gave valuable literary aid. Norman Cordes supplied a missing link by lending me his actual electrotyped matrices, and Merle Langley of Marlboro Mats also offered advice on how the electrotypes might have been made.

Dr. Wolfgang Kummer and David Dinin of the Linotype Company offered support in the hope that my final work would add new knowledge about the inventor. They also gave me access to the company's archives on Long Island, where with the help of Steve Byers and Joe Mazzella some scarce documents and photos turned up.

Some skilled graphic artisans who helped bring this work into being include Andy Schwartz, Victor Castellano and Wes Gaudiamo. Gene Maggio, Nestor Delgado and Fred Lugo, Jack Taromina and Dave Brown, Mike Rosen, Ted Elia and Nick Stachniak also extended themselves to help me.

A special nod goes to Jeannie Friedman, whose unpublished 1979 paper "The 15-year struggle between Typographical Union Local 6 and the New York Tribune" laid excellent groundwork for my study of the Whitelaw Reid papers nine years later at the Library of Congress.

If I have unintentionally missed mentioning any friend who has helped me, I offer my apologies in advance. I tried to keep track of all my conversations but no doubt slipped up somewhere. I especially owe appreciation to my wife Renée, who was there when I needed her to patiently offer me advice, which I took—most of the time.

Thanks, my love.

Now, on to the book.

September 14, 1988   CARL SCHLESINGER

The "Biography" of Ottmar Mergenthaler

by STEPHEN O. SAXE

Editor, American Printing History Association *Newsletter*

SOME YEARS AGO I bought a book titled *Biography of Ottmar Mergenthaler,* which contained no biographer's name, and though published in Baltimore, Mergenthaler's home, bore no publisher's imprint. I compared the book with a catalogue I owned that pictured Mergenthaler's Baltimore factory. Finding similarities in paper, binding and typefaces, I began to suspect the "biography" was more than that. At the New York Public Library no copy of the book still existed except on microfilm. When I began the reel, I found the title page inscription, shown on the page opposite this. At the reel's end I found the full page of writing, also shown opposite.

Mergenthaler knew he was dying. With his previous autobiography notes destroyed in a fire, he had but a short time to get his account of events before the world. He told his story to Otto Schoenrich, his children's tutor. Today we would call the work an autobiography, "as told to Otto Schoenrich." But however we describe it, it is, most importantly, Ottmar Mergenthaler's dying testament.

Transcription of handwriting on the flyleaf of "Biography of Ottmar Mergenthaler."
() = conjectured wording; the page is torn.

> When in 1898 my friend Mergenthaler returned from South Western New Mexico, where he had spent, with (his) family, about two years as a last means to be cur(ed) from consumption, he realized that he had only a short time to live yet–he had come home to di(e.) He, however, hoped to live long enough yet to have a manuscript printed which he had prepared with care, aided by my oldest son, so that, as he express(ed) it his friends and the world may get an authent(ic) history of his invention. My son, now a judge in ( ) River, was then the tutor of Mr. Mergenthaler's sons (and) during that time a member of his family; he at (that) time was practising law in the Territory of New Mexico.
>
> The book appeared in due time, Mr. Mergenthaler had about a thousand copies printed and distributed; this one the inventor handed to me two weeks before his death, and in order to make it accessible to a great many I hereby present it
>
> To the New York Public Library
> Lennox (sic) Library Bldg., Richard E. Helling, Librarian.
>
> Carl Otto Schoenri(ch)

Baltimore, Feb. 5, 1907

Transcription from the title page: (handwritten)

> Written during the winter of 1897/98 in Deming, New Mexico, under the direction and supervision of Mr. Ottmar Mergenthaler, by Otto Schoenrich, L.L.B., of Baltimore, Md.

xvii

The writing below was photographed from the microfilmed copy of the book at the New York Public Library. The original can no longer be found.

OTTMAR MERGENTHALER,
(Photograph, 1894)
THE INVENTOR OF THE LINOTYPE.

BIOGRAPHY OF

Ottmar Mergenthaler

AND

History of the Linotype,

Its Invention

AND

Development.

BALTIMORE, MD.
1898.

OTTMAR MERGENTHALER IN 1879.

BIOGRAPHY OF
MR. OTTMAR MERGENTHALER.

The subject of our sketch was born in the Kingdom of Württemberg, Germany, on May 10th, 1854, he being the third in a family of five children. His father, Johann Georg, was a teacher in the public schools, and his mother, *née* Ackerman, was the daughter of a teacher, whose ancestors had for generations been following teaching as a profession.

When young Ottmar arrived at the age of 14 he was to leave school and enter a seminary, where he too should receive his training as a teacher, but the boy was not in favor of this profession, and remembering that for years he had very successfully handled the rather rebellious village clock, and that he had done various work of similar nature, it gave him the idea that machinery was the thing he would feel most interested in. Instead of becoming a teacher, he now accepted an apprenticeship under the brother of his stepmother, Mr. Hahl, a watch and clockmaker at Bietigheim, Württemberg, a town of about 4,000 inhabitants.

In May, 1868, he began his apprenticeship, and applied himself to mastering the intricacies of the trade, with all the energy and enthusiasm he was capable of. At the same time the young man tried to advance himself mentally by attending the night and Sunday schools, and it was here where he received his first knowledge of mechanical drawings, which later on assisted him so much in his business, particularly in the drafting of his own inventions and designs.

In the fall of 1872, his term of apprenticeship having expired, the young man concluded to emigrate, and thereby avoid being drafted into the army, in which his two older brothers were already serving.

With the assistance of a son of his uncle, who some years previously had established electrical instrument works at Washington, D. C., Mr. Mergenthaler left his home, and landed in Baltimore in October, 1872, at the age of 18, and went on to Washington, where he arrived with a trunk well filled with clothing and with $30 cash in paper money.

He commenced work at once, and inside of two years took the leading place among his fellow-workmen at the Hahl shop. Besides the manufacture of electrical clocks and bells, his occupation consisted largely in work on the instruments used in the United States Signal Service. Many of the standard instruments were made at the Hahl shop, and most of the necessary experiments on them were carried out directly under the hands of Mr. Mergenthaler. It was a class of work he liked, and for which he showed a particular aptitude, both by his skill and ease of execution, as also for the readiness with which he understood the inventor's ideas. Washington was at that time the great center for all important inventions made not only in the United States, but all over the world. Mr. Mergenthaler came into daily contact with them, and inventors and inventions furnished the topic of conversation. With such surroundings the young man could hardly fail to develop his own inventive talent, and long before he was of age he had left the impression of his ingenuity on many a machine or instrument and was generally recognized as a mechanic of no ordinary ability.

In the course of time the Hahl shop was removed to Baltimore, and Mr. Mergenthaler, following the fortunes of his employer, went with him. With this we now come to the main subject of our writing, namely the commencement of work by Mr. Mergenthaler on machines which led to the invention of the Linotype as it is known to the printing world to-day. (For the invention of the Linotype proper see pages 11 and 13.)

THE EVOLUTION OF THE LITHOGRAPHIC ROTARY MACHINES.

It was one day early in August, 1876, that a gentleman called at the Hahl shop in Baltimore, introducing himself as Mr. Charles Moore, of West Virginia. He was the inventor of what he called a writing machine, and wanted to make terms for remedying its defective workmanship, to which he attributed the failure of his machine to work. As the financial sponsors of his invention he named Mr. J. O. Clephane, his brother Louis Clephane, Maurice Pechin and J. H. Crosman, all of Washington, D. C. Mr. Mergenthaler thoroughly examined the machine, and found that not quality of workmanship but errors of construction were the main causes why the machine did not perform what was expected. He gave the problem some serious thought, and soon saw his way clear to overcome some of its defects by remodeling the machine, and at the same time to simplify it greatly. He so informed Mr. Hahl, who thereupon contracted with the proper parties for the reconstruction of the Moore writing machine, guaranteeing to demonstrate the practicability of the plan, by making at least seven letters, including the widest and narrowest, print clear and sharp on a page of paper, and spacing each letter correctly in proportion to its width.

We may explain here that the general idea of Mr. Moore's machine was to produce by type-writing a print just like that produced from printer's type, the idea being to avoid the cost of type-setting, and to multiply the work so made by the lithographic process. The idea underlying this system was Mr. J. O. Clephane's, while Mr. Moore undertook to construct the necessary machinery. It is therefore Mr. J. O. Clephane, to whom justly belongs the honor of having furnished the abstract idea of producing print without requiring type composition, of finding men who carried his idea into practice, and of furnishing means and inducing men of means to carry on experiments through years of adversity, thus saving the enterprise from almost certain death on more than one occasion. We take pleasure in introducing here his likeness and a few words as to his personality.

James Ogilvie Clephane was born in Washington, D. C., February 21st, 1842, of Scotch parentage. Beginning the study of short-hand at an early age he soon took first rank in his chosen profession. All the important trials taking place at the National Capital during the time he was actively engaged in business were reported by him. Dissatisfaction with manuscript copies led him at an early date to take up the subject of type-writers, and, as Mr. Sholes, the inventor of the Remington type-writer, often said, it was the practical encouragement given by Mr. Clephane, and the severe, as well as the impartial criticism he gave regarding the machines, that really led to their perfection. At the same time he was urging forward other inventions in this line and expending large amounts of capital for the purpose.

About this time he was admitted to the Bar of the Supreme Court of the District of Columbia. He had several very tempting offers to enter actively upon the practice of law, but his interest in the inventions which he was fostering, became so great that he was reluctantly compelled to forego his inclination in that direction and devote his entire time to the perfection of the new printing process.

Reverting to our history, we find the remodeled Moore machine completed and performing all that was expected of it. Thereupon a full-sized machine was constructed by Mr. Mergenthaler, he making his own drawings and doing most of the machine work himself. The machine was finished in the summer of 1877, and, printing on an endless narrow strip, worked very rapidly; mixed composition could be done with great ease by means of a single shifting of the type wheel carrying Roman and Italic faces; the spacing of the letters seemed to be very accurate, and the print was sharp and clear. Everybody was delighted. But what a disappointment was in store for the parties interested! When they came to the final stage of the process, the lithographing, it turned out that the conditions underlying the lithographic process were far more exacting than any of the parties had had any idea of at the time they started. The stone failed to take all the impressions of the original copy; it often showed blurs where nothing seemed to be wrong with the original, and the work lacked sharpness and regularity of result. There were too many processes, a failure in any one of them resulting in entire failure, or at least, in greatly impairing the quality of the work. In the printing machine there

JAMES O. CLEPHANE,
THE FIRST PROMOTER OF THE LINOTYPE.

might be too much or too little ink used, the paper was not always properly covered with a starch coat, sometimes the paper caught oil while running through the machine, the operators would touch it with greasy hands, etc. The conditions governing the impressions in the composing machine were found to be most exacting, requiring simply a deposit of ink on the surface of paper and tolerating no impression in the paper at all. Add to this the possibility of failure in the transfer to the stone and the comparatively slow work of printing copies by the lithographic process, and we have a fair idea of the extreme difficulties implied in obtaining commercially satisfactory results from the system described above. It cannot be denied, however, that occasionally results were very satisfactory. Pamphlets and small books were printed; reporting offices were opened in Washington, Chicago and New York, and considerable commercial work was done in all of them, yet the system lacked the great requirement of trade, namely uniformity of product and uniformity of cost. Everything possible was done to improve the system, but the difficulties were too many, and finally even the persistency of Clephane and the ingenuity of Mergenthaler had to concede the fact that they had exhausted themselves, and that a change of system was the only way out of the dilemna.

THE CHANGE TO THE ROTARY STEREOTYPIC SYSTEM.

Conceding the many difficulties inherent in the lithographic method, Mr. Clephane now suggested changing the process by substituting stereotyping for lithographing, in other words, the construction of a writing machine which would impress its characters into papier-maché, and produce type from these matrices by the stereotypic process. The system of printing on narrow strips was to be maintained so as to be able to justify by cutting out between words, or in some other way which experience might suggest.

As usual, when a mechanical problem was to be solved, Mr. Mergenthaler was looked to for the solution. Up to this time he had never seen a stereotype nor did he know anything about the stereotypic process, but a short investigation in that direction made him doubtful of the practicability of the proposed plan, which prompted him to waive all responsibility in regard to the problem of making a satisfactory type from the matrices of his prospective machine. However, Mr. Clephane exclaimed, "Give us the impression machine and let me attend to the rest!" He assumed the whole responsibility for that part of the problem, and gave the order for the new matrix machine.

In the latter part of 1878 we find this machine completed. It made a matrix well spaced between letters, with sharp impressions, and which was apparently as good as an ordinary stereotypic matrix. Again, there were joy and enthusiasm in the camp of inventors, and again, they were doomed to disappointment by subsequent developments.

A casting mould had been simultaneously made with the stereotyper, and no time was lost in putting it to a test. The idea was to cast independent slugs or lines of type, and the mould consisted of a metal frame with cross pieces, between which the several lines were to be formed. The front of it was closed by the matrix and the back by a metal plate, and the mould was intended to cast about forty lines at a time. The first trouble encountered was that the metal would chill and not fill the mould at all, because of the many partitions in the latter. To get a casting the mould had to be heated to the temperature of liquid type-metal, and when so heated another trouble was encountered almost as bad as the original one. The metal now would not only fill the mould and matrix, but would also penetrate into every joint of the mould and every crack or pore in the matrix, thus destroying the matrix while it was being drawn from the type, and rendering the removal of the slugs from the mould very difficult and slow. Between many failures, now and then good castings were obtained; they were eagerly cleaned of burrs, and the paper sticking to their faces removed with brushes, pens, acids, fire, and other expedients too numerous to mention. Hours and half-days were thus spent, sometimes on a single page of printing matter, and yet the type was not clean. The papier-maché would stick to it with a tenacity that resisted everything. Press proofs, too, soon demonstrated the fact that the matrix machine did not produce the required accuracy as to height to paper, that is, the depths of the impressed letters varied according to the size and shape of the letter. The paper matrix also showed the existence of what was termed " interference," or in other words, a displacement of the material into the matrix made previously, which resulted in a distortion of the right side of each letter. Another difficulty encountered with the matrix machine was the necessity of keeping the paper properly moistened while being worked. Yet Mr. Mergenthaler succeeded in overcoming all these difficulties to a point where they were deemed to be no serious obstruction to the success of the system as a whole, though in the light of our present experience it is clearly evident that no really good printing could ever have been done from a matrix made by that process.

Shortly after completing the first rotary stereotyper Mr. Mergenthaler remembered that he had now been exercising his inventive ability for several years in the interest of a corporation, and had given it what at that time appeared some very valuable patents without the slightest compensation. Mr. Hahl, too, thought he had done more than his duties as a mere shop-owner called for, and both of them made a demand for some tangible recognition of their services. This demand led to a little misunderstanding, but after a few days the matter was satisfactorily compromised, and Mr. Mergenthaler received three shares of stock, equal to one-twenty-

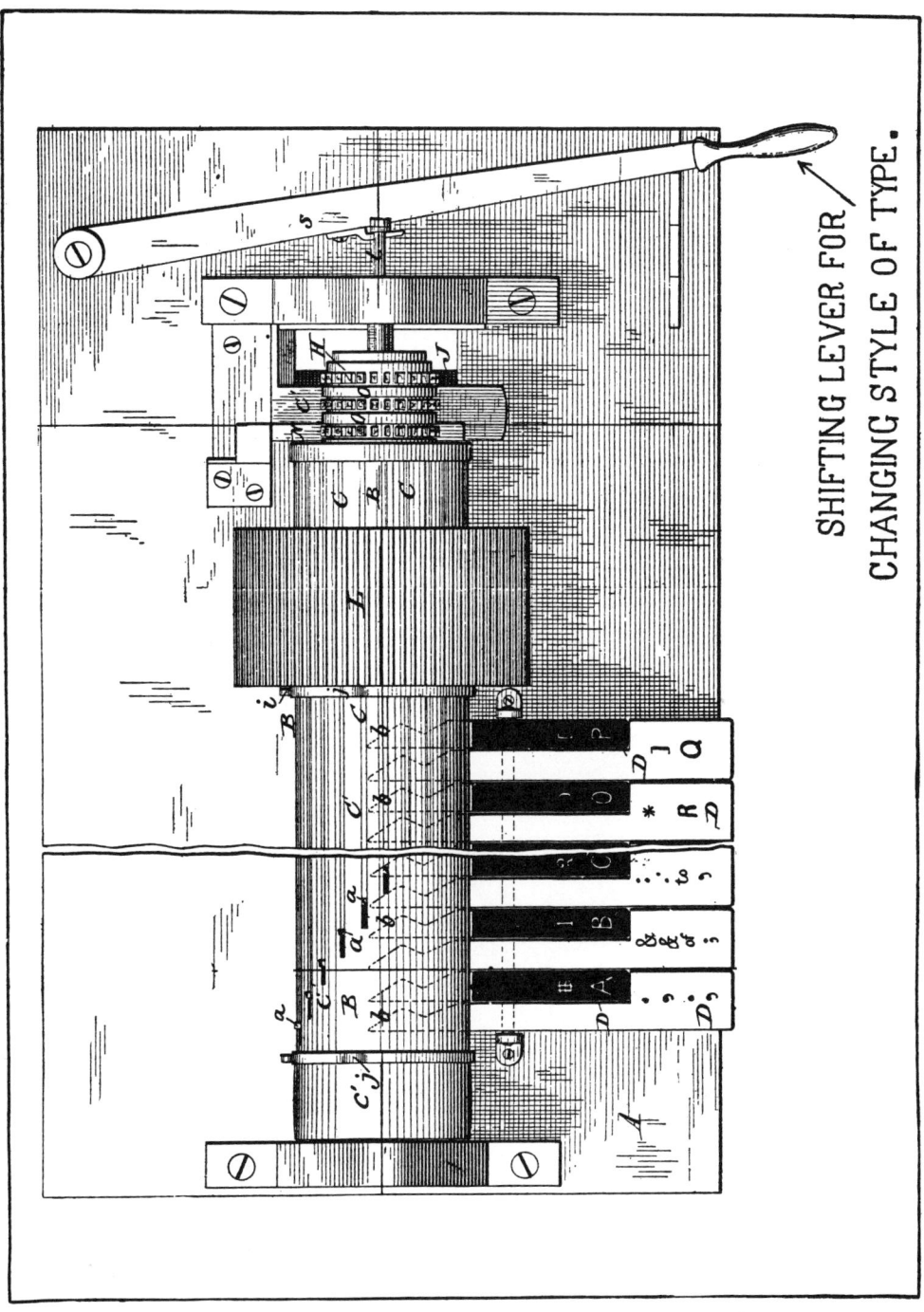

TOP VIEW OF ROTARY IMPRESSION MACHINE, 1879.
(Turn page sideways to view correctly)

fourth, as his interest in the company; a princely reward for his labors, considering that practically every patent on which the system depended was his invention. Mr. Hahl was accorded an equal interest, though it is not clear to this very day why he was thus favored, there being not a single patent or invention to his credit. After this settlement the problem was attacked with renewed vigor, and during the whole summer of 1879 the testing of the system and experiments looking towards the solution of the casting problem were kept up night and day in the Hahl shop, but in vain.

Mr. Mergenthaler now came to the conclusion that further efforts for the perfection of this system were useless, and so informed Mr. Hahl, and Mr. Clephane and his associates. The latter, however, were of a different opinion, and concluded to continue experiments. They removed the machine and appliances to Washington, and established a little machine shop of their own, where they worked honestly and persistently for years, but all to no avail. In spite of the ingenuity of Maltby, White, Moore and others, the system at the time of its final abandonment in 1884 showed no improvement over its condition when it left the hands of Mr. Mergenthaler in 1879.

From this time up to January 1st, 1883, Mr. Mergenthaler's connection with the enterprise ceased almost entirely, being confined to occasional calls at the Company's Washington establishment and a number of consultations with the leaders.

Recognizing the defects of the present system, Mr. Mergenthaler now for the first time attacked the problem as a whole, considering it in all its bearings, and leaving no part of it to the care of Mr. Clephane or anybody else, as had been the case in his first two efforts. He soon laid down a number of requirements as fundamentally necessary in a machine which would be able to statisfactorily solve the problem of producing cheaper composition without lowering its quality. The new plan called for the use of regular type as a means of getting perfect impressions into the matrix, and a fixed, invariable spacing between the letters. The impressions into the paper matrix were to be made line by line, and not letter by letter, as in the old system, so that the line might be justified automatically, and that interference and the irregularities of the impression caused by wide and narrow faced letters under the old system might be overcome.

The principles soon found expression in a drawing which he made towards the close of the year 1879. Before, however, completing this drawing he destroyed it in a fit of anger brought about by the extreme financial straits into which he and the Hahl establishment had gotten themselves by reason of their connection with the enterprise, for much of the late experimental work was carried on on credit, and there was often not one cent of money left in the treasury of the Company to pay for the work. To give an idea of the hopelessness with which Mr. Mergenthaler at that time regarded the chances of the existing stereotypic system, it may be mentioned here that in the summer of 1881 he sold his entire interest therein to a friend for the sum of $60.00. His partner, Mr. Hahl, some time later, after Mr. Hine's advent in the Company had infused new hope, sold his share for $900. To-day the value of these interests would amount to hundreds of thousands.

Up to 1882 the problem of providing funds to carry on the above named work devolved almost entirely upon Mr. J. O. Clephane, but about that time he succeeded in interesting in the enterprise Mr. L. G. Hine, a prominent lawyer of Washington, and from then on Mr. Hine became the recognized leader as well as the man who furnished the funds for the work of further development. It was a great strike on the part of Mr. Clephane, and if he had never done anything in behalf of the enterprise except interesting Mr. Hine in it, he would deserve on that account alone the lasting credit and thanks of its stockholders. In Mr. Hine the right man had been brought into the right place. He combined all the qualities essential for a leader in an embryo enterprise, being a man of sterling integrity, of commanding and confidence-inspiring appearance, not an enthusiast, but a man of rare persistency. Liberal almost to a fault, and always ready to give due weight to the opinion of those who, by reason of their special training and talent, were better qualified to judge mechanical problems, he, better than any one before or after him, understood the requirements of the situation and allowed the inventor that liberty of action which is so essential to success.

Under Mr. Hine new energy and fresh capital were brought into the Washington experimental shop. The established printing office was removed to far more pretentious quarters at the corner of Louisiana Avenue and Seventh Street, six new rotary matrix machines were ordered and delivered by a New York firm, new paging machines and other contrivances were made, more operators employed, in short, everything possible was done to develop the system into a commercial success, but in vain; yet, though days, months and years passed without progress, he kept on.

In the meantime Mr. Mergenthaler became a partner in the Hahl establishment, and in the fall of 1881 was married to Miss Emma Lachenmayer, which happy union has since resulted in the birth of five children, four boys and one girl, of whom four are living to-day, and constitute the pleasure and pride of their parents.

On January 1st, 1883, the partnership with Mr. Hahl was dissolved and Mr. Mergenthaler started a business of his own on Bank Lane, Baltimore, Md., and with this date his connection with the printing problem was re-established.

MR. L. G. HINE.

FIRST START OF THE LINOTYPE PROPER.

Messrs. Clephane and Hine had by this time seen enough of the old system to convince them that a change to something better would not be much out of place. Mr. Clephane had informed Mr. Hine of Mergenthaler's new system, and brought about an introduction between them with a view of making terms for the construction of a machine on the new plan, and as a result, early in January, 1883, an order for such a machine was given. In case of success Mr. Hine was to compensate Mr. Mergenthaler for his invention by giving him some fair share in the invention, the amount and time of adjustment of which were left entirely to the fairness of the former.

It will be seen from the foregoing that Mr. Hine undertook the development of Mr. Mergenthaler's plans on his own account, and not in the interest of the Company; it was Mr. Hine, Frank Hume, and Kurtz Johnson, of Washington, who, for quite a long time, paid for all the work done by Mr. Mergenthaler under his new plan, and the consolidation of the interests held by them in his latest invention with the interests represented by his former invention did not take place until January, 1884. Mr. Hine, being the owner of a controlling interest in the old system and absolute owner of the new one, had practically absolute power to consolidate or to keep the new system as his own separate property. He concluded to do the former.

The first thing to be made was a small experimental machine. It was capable of printing but twelve letters at a time, was very roughly made, and showed a good many defects, yet it demonstrated beyond a doubt that a complete working machine made on its principle would be an enormous step in advance of the old machine. This experimental machine was quickly followed by a full-size working machine, which was brought to a test as early as the fall of 1883.

The machine was a great success, yet severe tests soon developed the fact that even with all the known difficulties removed, there was still one difficulty to contend with, namely, the paper matrix itself, or, rather, the method of drying it. The ordinary stereotype process calls for drying the matrix while still on the face of the type, but in this case Mr. Mergenthaler had to remove it while wet, and dry it afterwards, because the speed with which the machine was to work precluded the possibility of leaving the matrix long enough on the type to admit of withdrawing the moisture from the former.

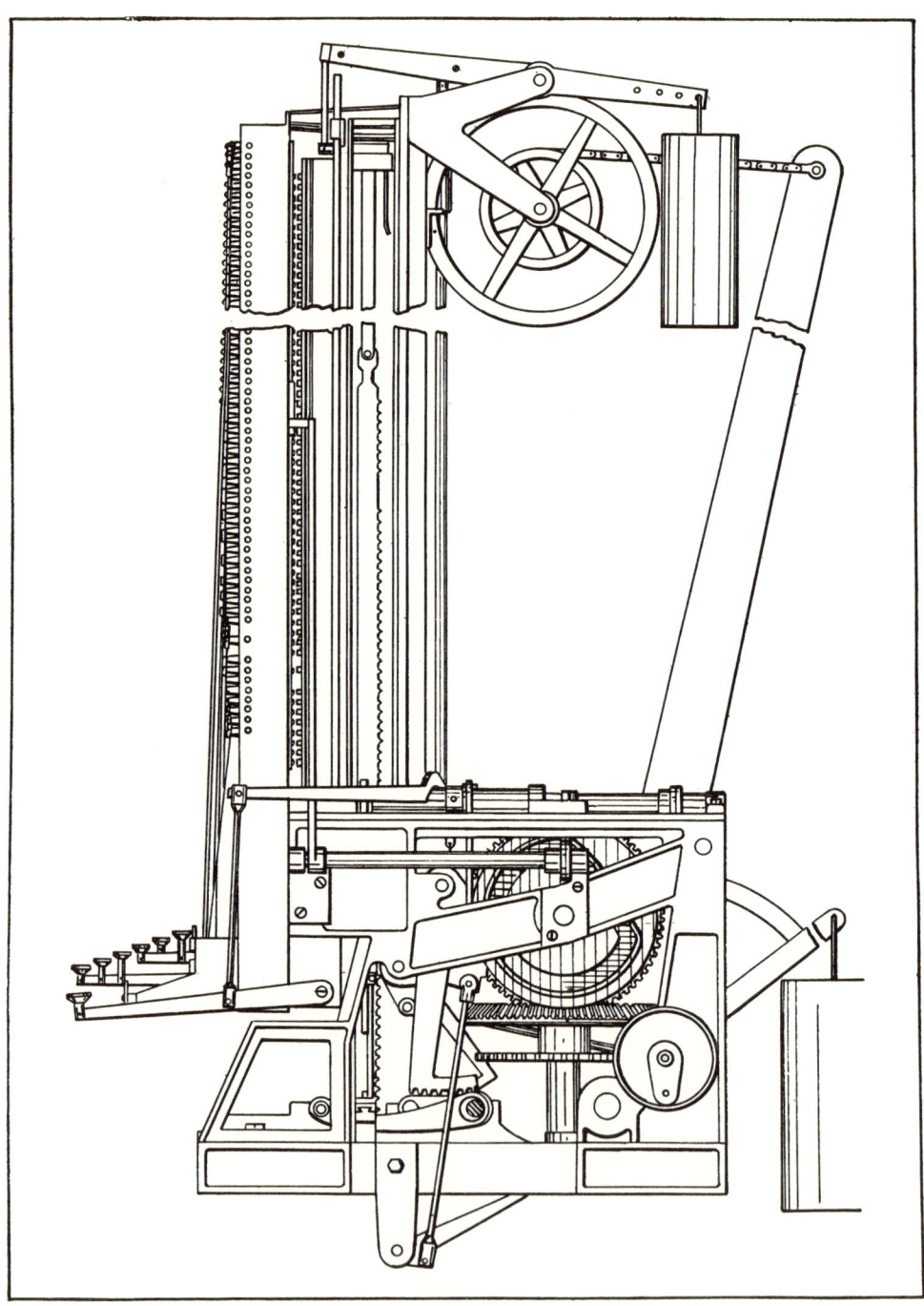

FIRST BAND MACHINE OF 1883.
(Note keyboard at left in this side view)

THE DIRECT CASTING MACHINE.

To overcome the obstacles of his latest machine, Mr. Mergenthaler soon came to the conclusion that only a metal matrix would fill the bill, but the use of metal as a matrix material would call for steel types, and these were almost out of the question when we consider that his latest machine contained 4500 types, and that each type would have cost $2.00. For weeks this problem was uppermost in the mind of the young inventor. The more he thought about it, the more he became convinced that he ought to have a metal matrix to secure the best results. Yet a metal matrix to be used like the old paper matrix was out of the question for reasons mentioned above. While matters were thus *in statu quo*, Mr. Mergenthaler was called to Washington for consultation with Messrs. Hine and Clephane. The subject, however, never left his thought, and while on the train going towards Washington, a new idea flashed across his mind. "*Why have a separate matrix at all; why can I not stamp matrices into my type bars and cast type metal into them in the same machine?*" Here we have the first idea of the combination of the casting and composing machine into one, and with it another important step in the advance of the art. The idea seemed to be perfectly feasible in every way. Surely the type metal would cool quickly enough to permit rapid working of the machine; surely, too, good matrices and cheap ones could be punched into the type bars, and the line could be justified by means of the wedge. On arriving at Washington no time was lost in convincing his associates of the importance of this his new and latest idea, and they could not find any pointed objection to it except that it seemed to be almost too bold to expect success, besides being so simple that if such a thing could be done, somebody certainly would have done it long ago. It was Columbus's egg over again, only in slightly different form.

Immediately thereafter Mr. Hine gave an order for two machines to be built on the line revealed by Mr. Mergenthaler's latest invention, and it was as early as July, 1884, that one of them was ready for trial.

The day of testing it was appointed, and at least a dozen interested spectators filled the little shop on Bank Lane. They had arrived several hours too early, and Mr. Mergenthaler had to do the finishing touches on his work in full view of a crowd of interested and more or less excited stockholders and their friends. He was sure of success and kept as calm and collected as he was accustomed to be on less momentous occasions. Finally everything seemed to be ready. He composed a line on the keyboard, then turned the driving pulley by hand, observing every action until the machine had gone through its full complement of duties and came to a stop. All was right. Mr. Mergenthaler now called for the steam power to be attached; he again composed a line, removed the stopper from the metal pump, and

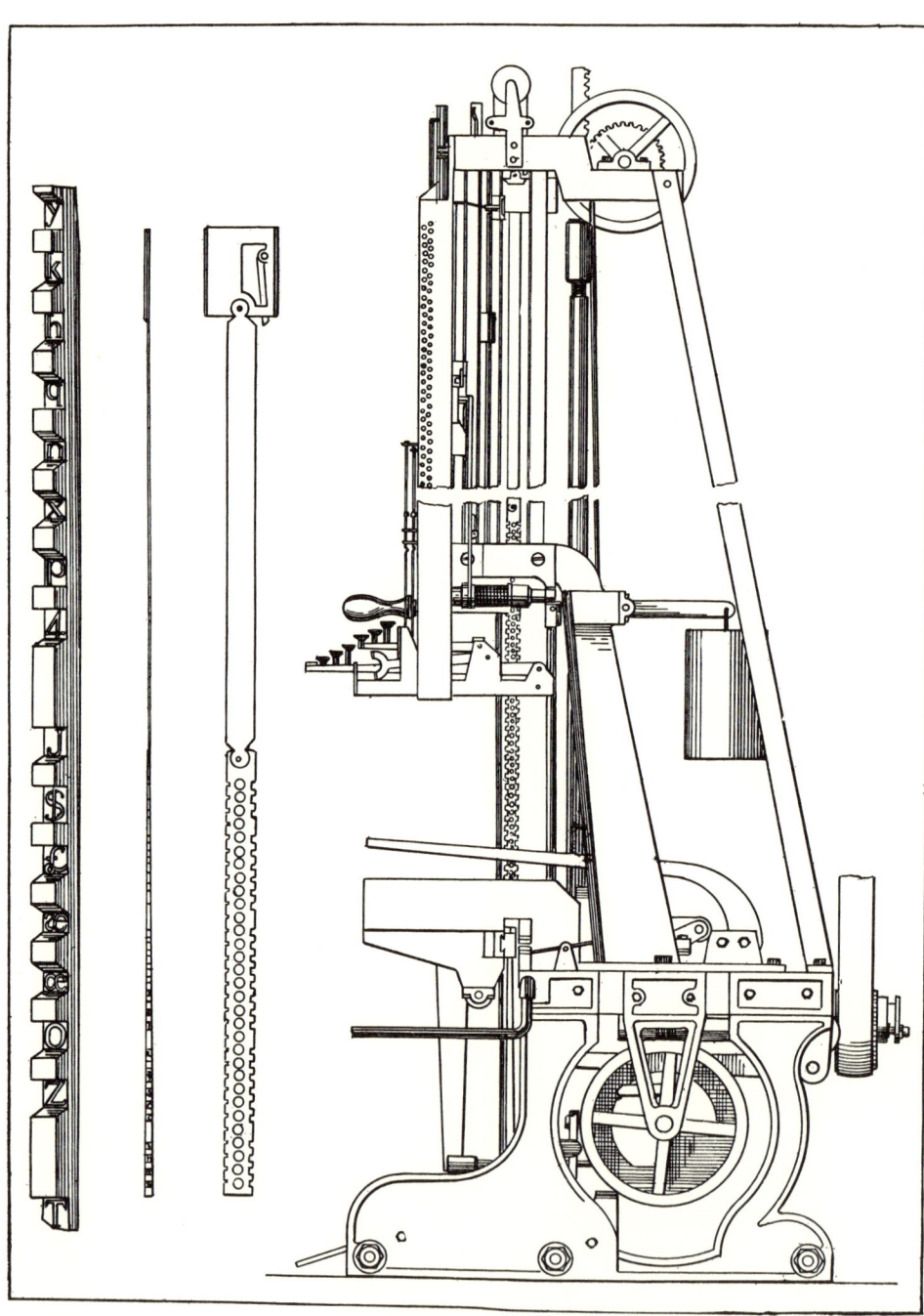

FIRST DIRECT CASTING BAND MACHINE OF 1884.

(Above: Three views of one of the matrix bands used in the machine.)

(Above: side view, keyboard at the left)

touched the line key. *Smoothly and silently the matrices slid into their places, were clamped and aligned, the pump discharged its contents, a finished Linotype, shining like silver, dropped from the machine and the matrices returned again to their normal positions.* All this was the work of but fifteen seconds. A few lines more made in this way by Mr. Mergenthaler, and the machine was turned over to Miss Julia Camp, a very gifted and rapid type-writer, who for years had wrestled with the lithographic and matrix making machines, always securing results superior to those of other operators.

The test proved a great success and everybody was delighted. For the first time a complete and finished type-line was produced by but one operator and but one machine.

We may state that in this machine the matrix letters were impressed on upright bands, each carrying a full alphabet, figures, etc., and the composing of the line was effected by allowing the bands to descend until they were caught at the proper elevation by stops, previously set up by operating the keyboard.

This first direct-casting Linotype had no automatic justification of the line, but the justification depended on the operator, who, with the assistance of a scale and pointer could see the length of the line before him, thus leaving it to his care to enlarge the spaces by striking the space key until the pointer indicated that the line was filled completely.

However, it was soon decided to apply the automatic justification by means of the wedge on the second machine, a method which Mr. Mergenthaler had already had in view for use for the first band machine in 1883, but which, on account of the higher cost, was not adopted. The cost of the machine at that time was to be below $400, and any machine calling for a larger expenditure of money was considered as not within the range of commercial success.

By this time a consolidation of the interests in Mr. Mergenthaler's late inventions and those represented by his labors between 1876 and 1879 had been effected, and a company organized under the name of "The National Typographic Company of West Virginia."

The latter now thought it desirable to establish a machine shop of their own, and Mr. Mergenthaler was requested to assume control of the proposed establishment, which request he finally consented to on the understanding that he should be sole judge of all mechanical questions, a condition without which he felt he could not do justice to himself and the Company.

In pursuance to the foregoing the Company established its machine shop in Baltimore, renting a suitable building at 201 Camden street. Mr. Mergenthaler's Bank Lane establishment furnished the nucleus of the new shop, and the Company added thereto a liberal line of the best tools and machinery.

The verbal understanding with Mr. Hine in regard to Mr. Mergenthaler's compensation for his inventions was now also shaped into a written contract, the substance of which was that while in the employ of the Company, Mr. Mergenthaler should have entire management and control of the Company's shops and factory; that all inventions or improvements which shall be made by him on the machines at any time thereafter, as well as before, shall be the property of the Company, and that in consideration therefor the Company shall pay him *ten per centum of the cost* of all machines manufactured by or for the Company, of which his invention or any of them may form a part. It was further agreed that only in case he should produce a machine fit for practical work the Company shall issue to him one thousand shares of its capital stock.

The reader will probably notice that **Mr. Mergenthaler's** share of his invention, promised under the terms of this contract, was small indeed; he will also notice that the main part of the same depended entirely upon his success in producing a commercially profitable machine. No money for the stockholders, no money for the inventor, is the substance of his agreement with the men who furnished the money. He did not object to these terms, but on the contrary, he advocated and favored them for the reason that he considered the whole future of the enterprise to depend on the confidence which he was able to command amongst those from whom the money came.

In the light of subsequent events it may well be claimed now that under any other agreement Mr. Mergenthaler's purpose in keeping on improving and superseding machine after machine with a still better one, would have been misconstrued and the impetuous money men would have compelled him to build machines for the public market long before his invention was ripe for it.

As it was, under the contract any delay in getting his invention upon the market was even more harmful to his own interests than to those of the general stockholder, hence in none of the many delays under which his invention had to suffer, did he lose the confidence of the stockholders, nor was his honesty of purpose doubted by them, in spite of the fact that for nearly two years he kept on improving the machine, when under their conception he ought to have manufactured machines for the market.

The agreement was a favorable one for the company, and it ought to have been a pleasure for them to comply with its terms when the time arrived to pay over to Mr. Mergenthaler his modest share in the shape of royalties on machines manufactured and introduced into use.

However, promises made by companies are only made to be broken, and men who, in their capacity as individuals, would be incapable of taking undue advantage of anybody, will at times resort to the most despicable methods when acting in the capacity of an officer of a company. Personal honor and the sense of personal responsibility are lost only too often, and their places are taken by a hollow pretence of duty to do their best for their company.

Future pages will show how the concern which profited millions and millions by his labors repaid Mr. Mergenthaler, and how even the foulest of means were resorted to to keep him out of his just dues.

Work was now pushed on as fast as possible, and in February, 1885, the second machine with automatic justifier was taken to Washington and there exhibited at the Chamberlain Hotel for several days.

The performance of the machine was generally commented upon as astonishing and almost superhuman in conception, and men like Secretary James G. Blaine, Hon. L. Q. C. Lamar, and others of equal prominence did not find it below their dignity to call and witness the operation of the machine; even Mr. Arthur, the then President of the United States, found time to witness its performance, and warmly congratulated Mr. Mergenthaler upon his work, expressing the wish that his splendid achievement might result in proper pecuniary reward for his labors.

The attendance at the banquet that followed the exhibition was of equal prominence, and under Mr. Stilson Hutchins' skillful leadership, who by this time had become a prominent stockholder and promoter of the Linotype, many an eloquent and witty speech was drawn from the lips of Senators and Representatives. During the course of the banquet Mr. Hutchins introduced the inventor, who was greeted with the heartiest cheers, and who, after quiet was restored, made the following little speech, which we herewith give to the reader, not as a sample of eloquence, but as the plain remarks of an inventor, showing the opinion he then held of the value of his invention, his hopes and prophecies for its future, and, last but not least, the cordial relations existing at that time between himself and the men who financially controlled his invention and who furnished the money for its development.

MR. MERGENTHALER'S SPEECH.

Allow me, gentlemen, to express my hearty thanks to you for the honor you have bestowed upon me in coming here to witness the performance of my invention. You have come here to witness the operation of a new composing machine, and in as far as we are working in a field which is strewn with the wrecks and failures of former efforts in the same direction you will probably ask, "Are you going to have more success than those who have gone over that field before you; and if so, why?" My answer is, "Yes, we are going to have full success for the reason that we have attacked the problem in an entirely different way than did those who have failed."

When I started on this problem I surveyed the field and selected the best road, regardless of the roads which others have taken. I knew the direction in which others had attempted to solve the problem, and was careful not to fall into the same rut which had led every previous effort into failure and ruin. We make and justify the type as we go along, and are thereby relieved from handling the millions of little tiny types, which have proved so troublesome to my predecessors who have failed. We have no distribution, yet we have a new type for every issue of a paper, an advantage which can hardly be overrated.

I am convinced, gentlemen, that unless some method of printing can be designed which requires no type at all, the method embodied in our invention will be the one used in the future; not alone because it is cheaper, but mainly because it is destined to secure superior quality.

The history of our enterprise, gentlemen, is one of evolution. We started by printing one letter at a time and justifying the sentences afterwards; then we impressed into papier maché one word at a time, justified it, and made a type from it by after process. Next we impressed a whole line and justified it, still leaving the production of the type as a second operation; but now we compose a line, justify and cast it all in one machine and by one operator.

It is a great result, but, gentlemen of the Board, to you it is due as much as to me. You have furnished the money, I only the ideas; and in thus enabling me to carry this invention to a successful end you have honored yourselves and your country.

I say you have honored your country, for every one will know that this invention has been originated in the land which gave birth to the telegraph, the telephone, the Hoe press and the reaper; everybody will know that it came from the United States, though comparatively few will know the name of the inventor. Gentlemen, again I thank you.

The speech was received with flattering applause, followed by general congratulations and hand-shaking with the inventor.

As stated before, the work of the machine was very satisfactory, yet not faultless. The matrix bands were not true enough and no tabular work could be done on it; correction of a mistake by the operator was impossible short of throwing away all that part of the line which had been composed to the time the error was discovered; and last, but not least, the operator could not see the result of his work before him as he touched key after key; in fact he produced no visible result at all, except an indication on a little scale or counter of the supposed aggregate width of the characters used in the line.

By this time Mr. Mergenthaler had become convinced that nothing would be able to overcome the prejudice of the printing trade unless the result produced was in every way equal to the result obtained by the use of ordinary type, and also that the method of composition should conform closely to that employed by the old-time compositor, in which the ability to read proof and correct his errors as he proceeds are the main features.

THE SINGLE MATRIX MACHINE.

Always active, and never satisfied until the highest perfection should be reached, Mr. Mergenthaler again set to work with a view of overcoming the shortcomings mentioned. The single matrix seemed to be the proper solution of the problem, for its adoption would cover every point mentioned as a fault of his last machine.

He soon gave form to the idea by settling the main features of his prospective machine, and this done, submitted his sketches to his financial backers, Messrs. Hine, Johnson, Clephane, and others.

It was a surprise to them, and a big one too, but not a pleasant one. The new idea called for the construction of an entirely new machine, and new machines were commencing to become odious to the promoters. As Mr. Hine expressed himself, "Not many stockholders can stand being told that we have the best machine in the world, but that we are going to make another which is still better."

Object as they may, they had to concede that the new idea, if capable of practical execution, would secure so many advantages that the manufacture of the existing machine had better be delayed until the new plan had been given a practical test.

Mr. Mergenthaler from now on devoted nearly his entire time to the plans for the new single matrix machine. The problem bristled with difficulties and, mechanically, was found much harder to press into practical form than the problems involved in his former machines. He had now to deal with thousands of matrices unconnected with the machine, yet being required to circulate through the same with rapidity and unerring certainty. In the act of depressing a key he had now to bring an actual matrix from the channel to the assembling point, and after the casting of the line the matrices had actually to be distributed very much in the same way as the compositor distributed his type.

However, as will be seen from later pages, Mr. Mergenthaler succeeded in overcoming all the difficulties involved in the new problem.

THE ADVENT OF THE SYNDICATE.

The next epoch of importance in the annals of the new invention is the advent of the syndicate, an association of wealthy newspaper men who interested themselves financially in the company by buying a controlling interest therein, for which they paid the enormous sum of over $300,000. The price paid was probably the highest ever paid in the United States for an interest in an invention which had never earned one cent, for the machine was not as yet introduced into a single printing office. The transaction caused general astonishment at the time, and served to materially increase the interest with which the invention began to be regarded by the printing trade and the public at large. The syndicate was composed of the following gentlemen: Whitelaw Reid, of the *New York Tribune;* W. N. Haldeman, of the *Louisville Courier-Journal;* Victor Lawson and Melville Stone, of the *Chicago News;* Henry Smith, of the *Chicago Inter-Ocean;* W. H. Rand, of Rand, McNally & Co., Chicago, and Stilson Hutchins, of the *Washington Post.* It was the idea of the original stockholders that by this transaction the introduction of the Linotype machine into the newspaper offices would be made as easy as possible, and that through association with these men, all of them representing large printing houses, the interest of the enterprise would be very materially advanced. In as far as a great deal of ill-informed comment has been published in the newspapers and periodicals of the United States regarding the supposed favorable influence of the syndicate in the company, it is but fair that the real facts of the case should be set before the public and no credit bestowed upon any one unless it was deserved.

Before the above named gentlemen invested in the enterprise, they and their agents paid several visits to the Camden street factory, where they were shown the operation of the machine. They were all very profuse in praise of the new invention and its future possibilities, but no one equaled Mr. Whitelaw Reid, who took special occasion to congratulate Mr. Mergenthaler and assure him of his desire to see him getting his proper reward, " not only by harvesting fame and glory, but also financially, adding thereto, that in case he and his parties should take hold of the invention it would be his particular aim to promote Mr. Mergenthaler's interest. He could already see him some day in the not too distant future returning to the fatherland a rich man, occupying with his family one of the noted and beautiful castles on the Rhine." Later pages will show how far Mr. Reid assisted Mr. Mergenthaler in securing his just dues, and how he was instrumental in acquiring for him that " castle on the Rhine."

The transaction was closed about May 1885, and one of the first changes made among the officers of the company was the substitution of Mr. M. E. Stone, of Chicago, for Mr. L. G. Hine, as chairman of the executive committee, thus substituting a new and inexperienced man as Mr. Mergenthaler's superior, in place of a gentleman, who by nature and years of experience, was better suited to deal with inventors and cope with the ever present difficulties incidental to any invention.

One of the first actions attempted by Mr. Stone was the removal of the company's workshop to Chicago, on the plea that he could not properly comply with his duties as chairman of the executive committee with the shop so far away from him. Mr. Mergenthaler did not feel very much like leaving a well established factory and all his friends and acquaintances for the uncertainties of Chicago. He could not see that Mr. Stone's nearness to the shop was in any way essential to the speedy development of the single matrix machine, and therefore politely but firmly declined to accede to the proposition.

HISTORY OF THE LINOTYPE 23

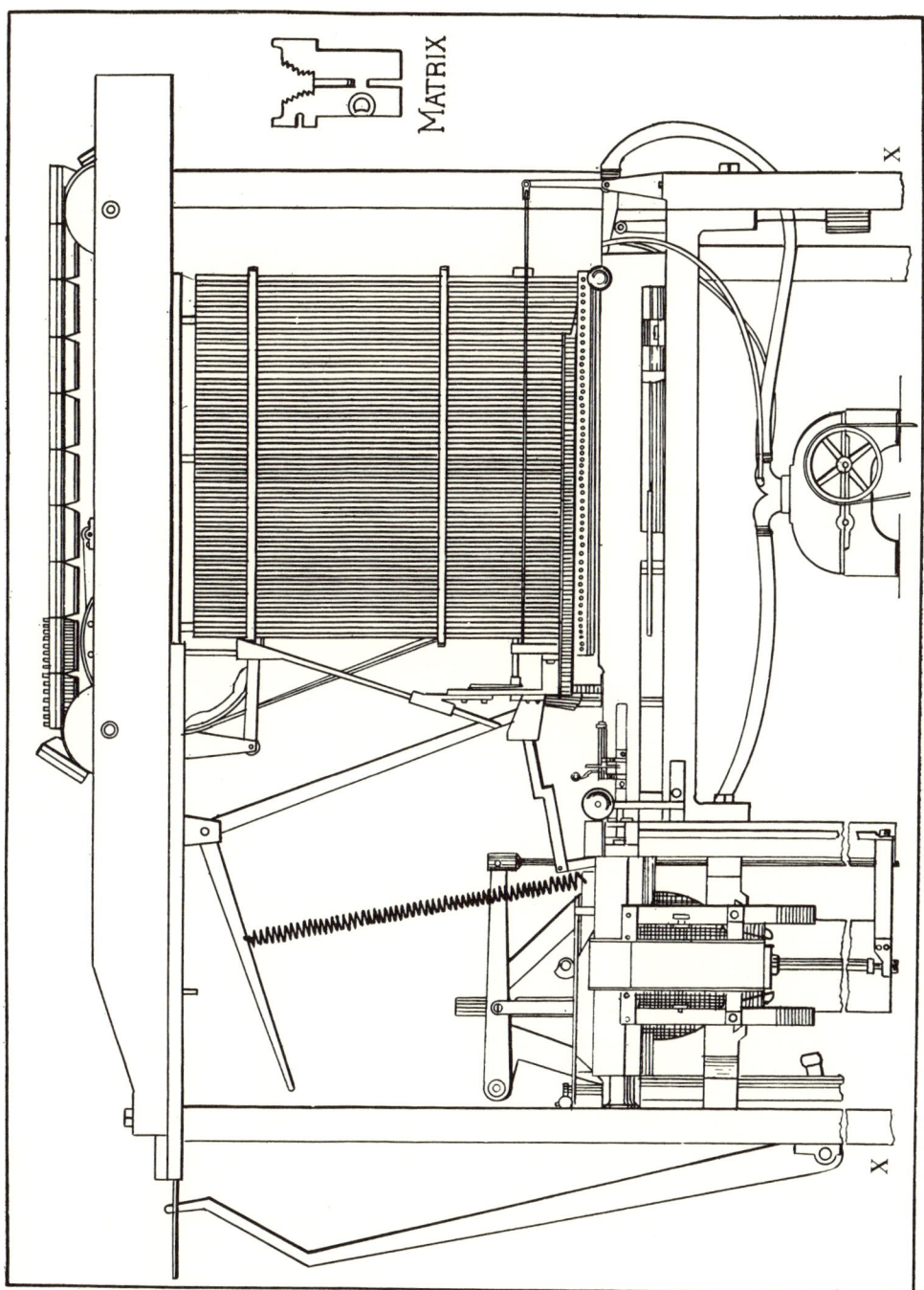

FIRST MACHINE WITH INDEPENDENT OR FREE MATRICES OF 1885.
(Turn page sideways to view correctly)

(Front view. "X"'s indicate legs of the machine.)
(For type sample set by this machine, see page 86)

The establishment remained in Baltimore, where Mr. Mergenthaler continued his work on the independent matrix machine, and had the satisfaction of bringing it to a satisfactory trial in the summer of 1885.

The machine now answered every expectation and every claim its inventor had made for it. The line was now assembled in full view of the operator, who could make corrections as he proceeded, and insert by hand italics or any other characters not carried in the machine; the machine could now produce tabular work; and the matrices, being independent of the machine and of each other, there was no limit as to the perfection to which they could be brought. All of the above named advantages were very readily noticed and appreciated by practical printers and compositors, and now for the first time this class of men commenced to give serious attention and consideration to an invention which for years had been carried on before their eyes without exciting more than ridicule or a disbelieving shrug of the shoulder.

THE ORGANIZATION OF THE MERGENTHALER PRINTING COMPANY.

The making of minor changes and improvements took up the time between its first trial and the first part of October, 1885, at which time it was thought that the machine was well enough developed to justify its manufacture on a large scale. The National Typographic Company, being organized with a fully paid up capital and non-assessable stock, had no funds with which to defray the heavy expenses implied by this resolution, and as a means of raising the necessary funds, it was decided to organize a new corporation under the name of The Mergenthaler Printing Company. Its capital stock of $1,000,000 was to be subscribed for, and assessments made up to the full face value of the shares if necessary. The Mergenthaler Printing Company was to assume full charge of the business and be entitled to one-half the net profits arising out of it, the other half going to the National Typographic Company. In practice the plan amounted to an assessment on the stockholders of the National Typographic Company, each stockholder being allowed to subscribe for an amount equal to his holding in the old company, any amount not covered by the original stockholders to be divided between such members as would be willing to take it. It was thought at the start that quite a large number of the smaller Washington stockholders would not feel like subscribing for their quota, with the risk attached thereto of being assessed up to the face value of their holdings, and that therefore the bulk of the new stock would go to the syndicate and the few large Washington holders.

However, Mr. L. G. Hine, the president of the National Typographic Company, foresaw the danger implied in this state of affairs, and used every means possible to induce the large army of small Washington stockholders to subscribe for the new stock. In a circular to them he said: "It is not thought that more than twenty-five per cent of the capital will ever be called for." His argument was effective, and the small holders subscribed nearly to a man for the full share of their holdings. Mr. Mergenthaler himself, who owned 1,000 shares of stock in the old company, found himself seriously embarrassed by the option thus offered to him. His position as inventor morally compelled him to share the risks of the other stockholders, and his influence in the company was thought to depend largely upon his doing so. Yet he was entirely unable to meet the assessment amounting to $25,000; his entire fortune, outside of the above named shares, at that time amounting to only about $8,000, and this was locked up in a dwelling house and his shop equipment, upon which he could not realize. An appeal to the directors of the newly organized company to accept his subscription and allow him to pay it later out of royalties which would accrue, was refused on the pretext that there was no authority in law for the board to grant the favor asked. Finally Mr. Whitelaw Reid volunteered to pay Mr. Mergenthaler's assessment, on the condition that he receive the stock as security, together with an irrevocable proxy, and that six per cent interest be paid on all money thus advanced. Reluctantly Mergenthaler had to accept, though it hurt his pride considerably to be thus thrown upon the generosity of an individual member of the company, particularly so, as Mr. Reid was to be the President and General Manager of the new organization, in which position he was Mr. Mergenthaler's immediate superior.

Funds were now plentiful and Mr. Mergenthaler was told that time was more valuable than money and that he should push matters with all possible energy and without undue regard for economy. The first thing to be done was to revise the working drawings with a view of taking as much advantage as possible of existing material and manufacturing facilities. So far, Mr. Mergenthaler had always made his own working drawings, but it now being the intention to manufacture the machines on a large scale he asked for the services of a professional mechanical draftsman with the idea that such a man could revise the drawings quicker and better than he could himself, who was neither a professional draftsman nor had had much experience in manufacturing on a large scale. His request was granted at once, for it promised what was wanted so badly, namely, a saving of time.

The selected gentleman, Mr. Sumter Black, came very well recommended and started to work at once. After the lapse of a week or so he, in course of conversation with Mr. Mergenthaler, passed a remark from which it appeared that he thought the job before him would take at least six months or more. "What!" exclaimed Mr. Mergenthaler, "six months to revise these drawings? Why I have made the first drawings inside of six months myself and have built the machine too." "Yes," replied Mr. Black calmly, "you have done it, but I can not, nor can anybody else. You are the inventor of this machine and of course you could reduce your ideas to paper quicker than anybody else. Besides, your drawings have not many details shown and comparatively few measures given. This will all do very well for one machine, but now you want to build many and employ a large number of hands on them. In order to do this successfully, you want to have perfect and complete drawings with all parts shown in detail and every measure indicated." Mr. Mergenthaler had enough practical experience to see the force of this argument, and although it implied quite an unexpected delay, he allowed Mr. Black to proceed on the lines he had laid down, and he was never sorry for it, for as the work progressed it developed that even the revised and detailed drawings were not any too complete nor too specific.

It was the intention of the board to give an order at once for one hundred machines, but Mr. Mergenthaler earnestly objected to the enormous risk involved in such an order, and finally the board consented to diminish the number to meet his views by reducing the first order to twelve machines. In July, 1886, we find the first one of these machines completed and at once forwarded to the composing room of the New York Tribune, where it was used on the daily paper and also on a large book called, "The Tribune Book of Open Air Sports," which book was composed entirely by this first linotype machine that ever went into commercial use. Other machines followed rapidly, so that by the end of 1886 most of the machines made under the first order were completed and at work in the Tribune composing room. The machines worked fairly well, but as usual with new machines some difficulties were experienced, partly due to weak or defective points in the machine, but more generally caused by the inexperience of both the operators and the machinist in charge. In the meantime, the board of directors had given orders to proceed on the construction of an additional lot of one hundred machines. This order was given at a time when there was but one of the first twelve machines delivered to the Tribune composing room, thus staking at least $130,000 on the result of but one machine obtained by an operation of only a few weeks' duration. Mr. Mergenthaler again protested and tried to have the board reduce the number to twenty-four, but in vain. The board decided that the machine was satisfactory to them and Mr. Mergenthaler had to yield.

Further experience with the first twelve machines convinced Mr. Mergenthaler that quite a number of improvements could and ought to be made on the one hundred machines then under construction, but here the board again interfered with his better judgment, and in the spring of 1887 unanimously decreed that the machines delivered to the Tribune composing room were satisfactory and enjoined him from

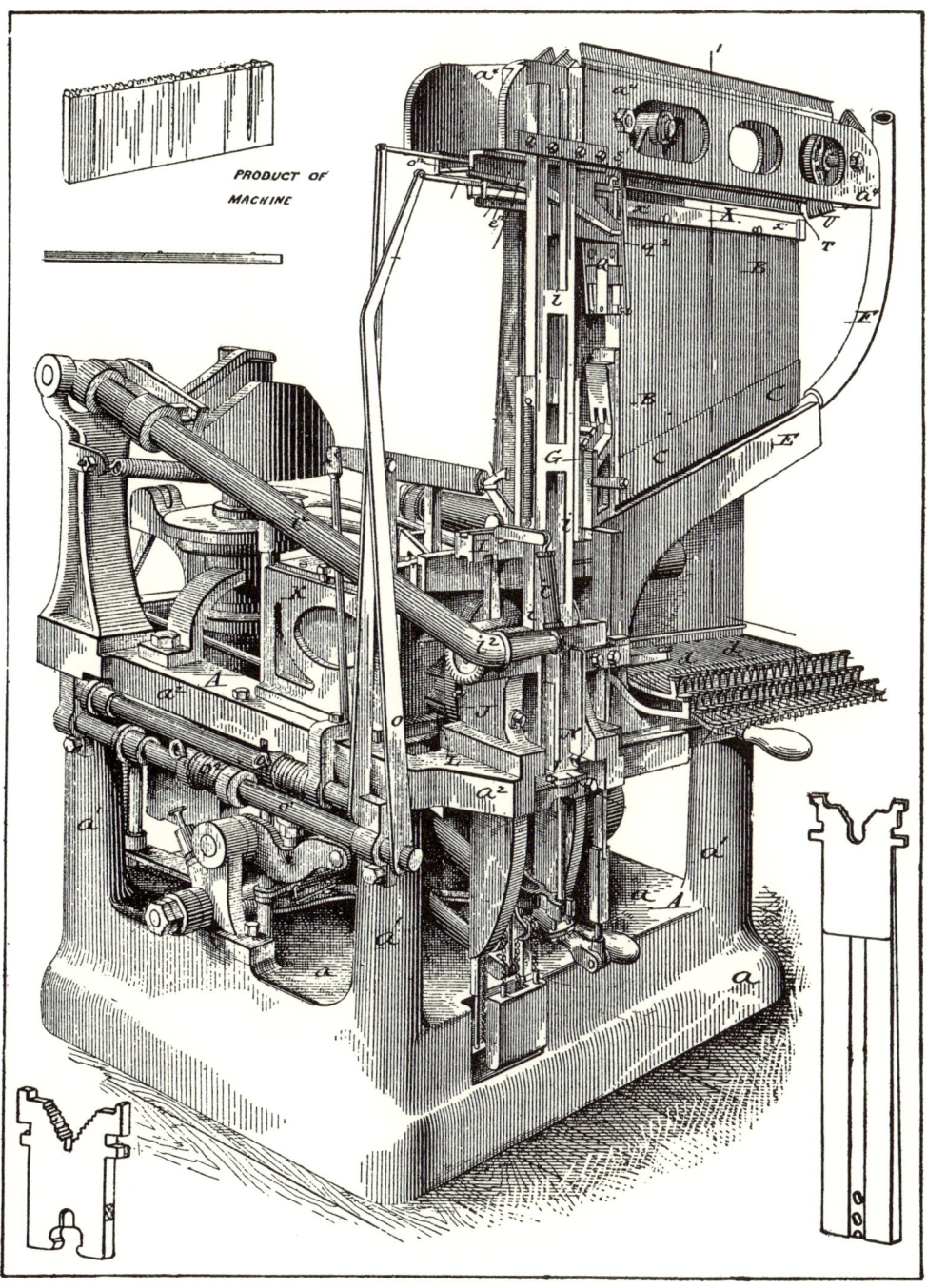

TRIBUNE MACHINE OF 1886.

carrying into effect any of the changes or improvements he then had in view. As a further demonstration of their unbounded faith in the machine of the kind first placed into the Tribune office it may here be recorded that before any of the one hundred machines were completed, the same board, composed nearly entirely of syndicate members with Mr. Whitelaw Reid as President, ordered another one hundred machines to be made like them, thus risking the cost of two hundred machines, representing an expenditure of about $260,000, all on the experience gained from the results of twelve machines. Mr. Mergenthaler pleaded for more conservatism, he implored them, he protested, and he predicted trouble in handling such enormous numbers simultaneously at the composing rooms, but all to no purpose, the syndicate members had matters their own way and used the results obtained with the twelve Tribune machines as an argument for their action just in the same way as Mr. Mergenthaler used these same results and experiences as an argument that further improvements, or at least further and more extended experience, were necessary to justify the enormous expenses incurred in the construction of more machines. It will readily be seen that no time could possibly be gained in giving orders for hundreds of machines at a time.

There was no shop organization existing at that time, there were no special tools, no means of testing the work for its accuracy, and worst of all, there were no linotype machinists and nobody who had ever seen or made such a thing. All these things had to be created first, and in manufacturing such large numbers of machines at a time, whatever errors were made affected the whole lot of two hundred, instead of two dozen, as would have been the case under Mr. Mergenthaler's proposed plan. However, it was the will of the board and Mr. Mergenthaler honestly tried to make the best of it. The plant at the Camden Street factory was much enlarged, and inside of a few months the number of men employed there was increased from about forty to one hundred and sixty. Shortly thereafter another building was rented on Preston Street and devoted exclusively to the making of matrices and the assembling of machines, in which place also over one hundred hands found employment on linotype work. Contracts were given to Detrick and Harvey, of Baltimore, for the framework of the machines, and to Garvin & Co., of New York, for some of the other larger parts, thus confining the company's own works to the making of the matrices, the production of the more delicate machine parts and the assembling of the machines. It was a Herculean task that confronted Mr. Mergenthaler. He not only had to design any number of special tools, but he also had to educate and instruct a force of employees entirely inexperienced in the special line in which they had to render their services. Add to the above the anxiety of the stockholders and executive committee for quick results and the reader can form an idea of the unenviable position in which Mr. Mergenthaler found himself during that period.

Probably the most difficult problem connected with the first manufacturing attempts was the production of the matrices at a price not prohibitive. Attempts to have them made outside under contract failed entirely. To give an idea of the discouragement he met with in these attempts the following incident may be mentioned. Mr. Mergenthaler, with a view to enlist outside help, called upon Mr. J. Ryan, a well known type-founder in Baltimore at that time. He showed him some of his matrices and told him that the machine required about twelve hundred of them and that they had to be produced at a cost not exceeding six cents apiece. Mr. Ryan took a look at his matrix, commenced to laugh, and said: "Young man, you see this matrix. It is one of our standard matrices and as you see it is a much simpler piece of work than yours. Now, we pay from fifty cents to a dollar apiece for the work of adjusting it after the impression has been made. If you can produce these matrices for the type founders at fifty cents apiece, there is a fortune in store for you on that line alone and you need not waste your energy in useless attempts to make impossibilities. Assuming that your machine as such is a success, yet it is bound to fail on the cost of the matrices if for no other reason." Similar answers were received from other sources and there was nothing left for Mr. Mergenthaler but to go ahead boldly and solve the problem himself. It required some thirty special machines and machine attachments to get up the required plant, and Mr. Mergenthaler for months devoted nearly his whole time to this part of the business, and after a while had the satisfaction of seeing the plant turn out matrices at a cost entirely satisfactory to all. The production of matrices on a commercial scale was a great achievement and the plant soon became the pride of Mr. Mergenthaler.

A great number of special tools and devices were also made for the Camden Street factory and the ingenuity and boldness displayed in some of them were admired by everybody who saw them. The editor of a Baltimore daily paper, after seeing the linotype and the means employed in producing it, expressed himself to the effect that the ingenuity and energy shown in the organization of the factory were second only to that shown in the construction of the machine itself, and that he could hardly conceive it possible that the two factories in Baltimore should have been created and equipped in so short a time. One great difficulty in the matrix department was found to be the expense and trouble of maintaining the original steel stamps which produced the matrix proper. There was no machine existing at that time by means of which these stamps could be engraved at a small cost with an absolute certainty of maintaining the same size and shape, but they had to be engraved by hand at a cost of $5 per piece, and their accuracy as a matter of course was far inferior to those later produced by the Benton & Waldo type engraver. Without the help of this machine it may well be said that good matrices as we now have them would be an impossibility. Mr. Mergenthaler soon discovered the need for such a machine, and failing to find anything in the market, he at once went to work designing an engraving machine. The work on this machine had already well advanced when the above named parties brought out theirs, thus causing work on his design to be discontinued.

It is a great pity that the above named machine did not come into the market a few years earlier. As it was, the first machine arrived after Mr. Mergenthaler's direct connection with the shop management had ceased, and too late to be of any service in his efforts to produce a higher quality of matrices.

As might well be expected a great deal of time was consumed in getting up the necessary tools and machinery, and in the selection of employees who would give any promise at all of becoming useful and efficient. The contractors too, Garvin & Co. and Detrick & Harvey, were behind time with their work, and when they finally commenced to deliver, it was found that considerable defective work had entered into their delivery, thus bringing in a new but not unexpected trouble. Mr. Mergenthaler now found himself between two dilemmas. If he accepted the defective work he could not expect the parts to be easily assembled into machines and there would be delay on that account, while if he did not accept it, it was a matter of many months to have new ones made and the delay would be worse.

Meanwhile time had passed rapidly and the spring of 1887 still found no finished machines out of the first lot of one hundred. The patience of Mr. Reid and his associates commenced to become exhausted and Mr. Reid's almost daily letters became what might be called one great and continuous jeremiad of complaints about slow results. Mr. Mergenthaler was told that the board might see itself compelled to go outside and contract for machines which could not be procured through him; that while they all appreciated his efforts very much, yet the fact could not be denied that hundreds of thousands of dollars had been expended, with only the first twelve machines to show for it; that the board did not believe that he was the only one who could make these machines; and many other things which were not at all pleasant to hear for the man who had invented the machines and who had strained every nerve to produce them as rapidly as possible. To make matters worse, Mr. Reid commenced to encroach upon the rights and duties of the factory manager, and under the pretence of relieving the latter of some of his arduous duties made appointments, increased wages, and otherwise interfered in shop matters without consulting Mr. Mergenthaler at all, thus rendering his position almost untenable. Amongst other incidents of this kind it may be mentioned here that Mr. Reid himself found the matrices in the first twelve machines then running at his office so unsatisfactory that he demanded new matrices to be made and threatened to stop the machines at his office unless the improved matrices could be produced within a short time. Mr. Mergenthaler, not being satisfied with the foreman in charge of the matrix department, now found himself compelled to discharge him and employ another one who would be more willing to be guided by Mr. Mergenthaler's orders as to the standard of correctness required in this work. Instead of endorsing Mr. Mergenthaler in his efforts to raise the matrix department to a higher level of efficiency, Mr. Reid re-employed that same man, raised his wages and established a special shop for him where he was to make matrices in competition with the Baltimore establishment.

This little side-show was kept going for years and never produced matrices which were used for more than a few days. In another instance Mr. Mergenthaler had in one of the factories a clerk who frequently showed himself under the influence of liquor and neglected his work. He being a brother of a prominent stockholder, Mr. Mergenthaler did not want to be harsh with him, but politely told him that he had to do better in future. To his great astonishment and disgust, a few days afterwards an order was received from New York in which this same man was given an independent tenure of office under the board and his wages were increased by the same body. He was now no longer under Mr. Mergenthaler's orders, but an independent employee of the board of directors, and in that capacity commenced to write regular weekly reports about the progress of work, a subject for which he was entirely incompetent.

The next great difficulty to be encountered in the manufacturing operation was the assembling of the machines. As mentioned before, the work of the contractors was deficient in many respects, but on account of the pressure for machines but little of it could be returned. Then, too, there were no facilities nor special appliances for testing the parts received, so that in many instances it was simply impossible to tell whether or not the parts were correct, from the fact that a careful measuring of the many dimensions would cost nearly as much as the making of the parts themselves. Of course, the most important test gauges were made and used to advantage, but the employment of a complete set was out of the question for the simple reason that there was no time to make them. The above named conditions in themselves were enough to cause serious delay and trouble, but if we add to them the fact that these machine parts had to be entrusted into the hands of machinists who almost to a man had never seen a linotype machine, the difficulty may then be appreciated in its whole extent.

Mr. Mergenthaler did all that was possible to assist and instruct this assembling force, he issued printed instructions, he remained with the men from early in the morning until late at night, he found the errors and defects and showed how to rectify them, but in spite of all, progress in the assembling room was slow. He now tried to secure better results by employing a higher class of labor for this purpose, and quite a number of toolmakers, mostly from the eastern States, were employed at wages varying from $3\frac{1}{2}$ to $4\frac{1}{2}$ dollars per day. There was never a more skillful and more intelligent set of men in any shop than these men were, but as assemblers of linotype machines they proved to be a worse failure than the ordinary machinists. They could not comprehend the many actions which these machines had to perform, and utterly wasted their time on things immaterial and neglected the points which were essential and important. Some few men out of the old force had become fairly efficient and assembled machines at a reasonable cost, but the cost of the work in the majority of cases was so much out of proportion that Mr. Mergenthaler concluded that something would have to be done to stimulate the energy of the men and if possible reduce the cost of the work to the company, besides giving wages to the men more in conformity with their services in that particular line of business. As it was, some men would assemble a machine for $40, while others would make the same work cost $250. Yet under the ordinary system of daily wages, this condition of affairs was unavoidable, for the learners insisted on receiving their accustomed daily wages just the same as those who had already mastered the intricacies of the machine. Some men would conceive easily and do fairly efficient work almost from the very start, while others apparently equally bright would take months to reach the same point of efficiency.

With a view of encouraging the more efficient men and in order to get out of them as much work as possible, Mr. Mergenthaler now introduced what was called the bonus system, under which every assembler was entitled to a bonus of $10 for every machine satisfactorily assembled and accepted by the company, always provided that the total cost of assembling did not exceed a certain amount. Under this system the efficiency of the assembling force increased rapidly and the cost of assembling was reduced wonderfully. One of the men soon managed to assemble two machines per week, thus giving him $20 extra pay besides his ordinary wages. Yet, the machines assembled by him cost far less than those assembled by any of the others. The system having proved a success on the assembling floor, Mr. Mergenthaler now introduced contract work in the manufacturing department too, and soon the efficiency of that branch increased wonderfully and the work was brought out much cheaper without in any way lowering the quality.

In the meantime the summer of 1887 had passed, and the delivery of machines out of the first hundred lot was progressing with a rapidly increasing output. By February, 1888, over fifty machines had been delivered to the

New York Tribune, Louisville Courier-Journal, Washington Post and Chicago News, and the balance of that lot was so nearly completed that by March the rest would have been ready for delivery. Not only this, but the second lot of 100 machines was so far advanced that by July of the year the whole of that lot would have been finished and delivered, as was evident from the actual rate of deliveries made of late. Mr. Mergenthaler had now brought up the efficiency of the factory to a point when it could have been relied upon to easily fill the demand for machines, and if left alone at least two hundred a year would have been the output from that time on. However, the syndicate did not want it that way.

THE BALEFUL WORK OF THE SYNDICATE.

The first intimation of impending trouble was given at the yearly meeting of stockholders in January, 1888. At that meeting Mr. Reid, in his capacity as President and General Manager, reported to an audience of at least 100 stockholders that so far the linotype machine had not proven itself to be the labor-saving machine it was supposed to be, and that, far from being a money maker, it had so far brought nothing but trouble, loss and disappointment to those using it, concluding his report with the statement that the syndicate members were ready to discontinue the use of the machines at any moment. This announcement was like a thunderbolt out of a clear sky. So far Mr. Mergenthaler, who more than any one else was in a position to know the actual facts, had seen nothing which in any way, shape or manner would justify so damaging a statement as the one made; on the contrary, the introduction and working of the machines so far delivered were progressing as smoothly as could be expected from new machines working under the hands of green operators and inexperienced machinists. More than that, Mr. Mergenthaler had dozens of letters from Mr. Reid and the foreman of his composing room which claimed precisely the reverse of Mr. Reid's report regarding the result of the use of the machines on the New York Tribune, not to speak at all of the prohibition of further improvements, which order was still in force against Mr. Mergenthaler. In the interest of truth and fairness Mr. Mergenthaler felt himself compelled to contradict Mr. Reid's statement in open meeting and call his attention to its variance from reports sent to Mr. Mergenthaler by Mr. Reid or by his foreman.

From this time on the relations between Mr. Reid and Mr. Mergenthaler became more and more strained, and more and more the former encroached upon Mr. Mergenthaler's special rights and privileges reserved to him under his contract with the National Typographic Company. Their opinions, too, as to the best policy to be followed by the company for the future, seemed to have undergone a complete reversal. So far, Mr. Mergenthaler had always counseled moderation as to the number of machines to be built, while the syndicate forced him to build hundreds. Now, after experience had been gained on larger numbers, Mr. Mergenthaler saw nothing discouraging in the result and advocated going ahead, while the syndicate claimed the machines to be worthless and commenced to make arrangements to stop work, thus threatening to disrupt the company's manufacturing facilities, the establishment of which was the result of years of hard work by Mr. Mergenthaler and which had cost thousands and thousands of dollars to bring to the efficiency they had then reached. In the line of orders, too, their position was now reversed. Formerly Mr. Reid kept pressing Mr. Mergenthaler for machines regardless of cost, now Mr. Reid failed to supply him with orders for the machines he had ready for delivery. Formerly Mr. Reid did not care for the cost of carrying out his orders, but now he became very economical and entirely forgot that nearly all of the extraordinary expenses had been incurred in an honest effort to carry out his own wishes. His letters more and more showed that Mr. Mergenthaler was not the man he now wanted in the place, and the latter of course took notice of this condition of affairs and seriously commenced to think of resigning a position which he could no longer fill satisfactorily to the syndicate management.

Under the contract and bonus system which Mr. Mergenthaler had introduced some of the contractors had doubled and trebled their ordinary wages, as was quite natural, while others had lost money, which was equally natural. Mr. Reid did not now consider the fact that the contractors had as many as twenty men working for them and that really the money which they earned amounted to but very little per day for each man employed by them. He forgot that the company was an enormous gainer by getting the work quicker and much cheaper than before, all he could see was the fact that certain men had been allowed to treble their wages and he set about censuring Mr. Mergenthaler unsparingly, as will appear from the following letter:

On February 25, the President and Chairman of the Executive Committee, who had already been urging Mr. Mergenthaler to avoid beginning new work, and thus to reduce his pay roll if possible, wrote to him as follows:

"After consultation with a considerable majority of the Board of Directors, I have found it the unanimous opinion that no steps should be taken towards the manufacture of a third set of 100 machines in Baltimore until the company are able to see their way more clearly out of what has already been undertaken, the completion of the second 100 and of the 41 still remaining on the first hundred. The reduction of the pay roll, instead of being the calamity you seem to consider it, would be regarded as a real advantage by the Board of Directors, and it is desirable that in doing it you should weed out the least useful men. * * * My earnest advice to you is to endeavor to reduce the expenditures in all these particulars to the most economical basis."*

The correspondence following the above letter is herewith given in full and will best explain itself. As will be seen, the consequence of it was Mr. Mergenthaler's resignation on March 15th, 1888.

In his reply, dated February 28, Mr. Mergenthaler said:

"The conclusion arrived at regarding the work in the Baltimore factories must certainly be considered as most distressing and injurious to the interest of the company. If the policy outlined is to be adhered to, it will amount to an almost entire suspension of the Camden street shop and the consequent loss of the most intelligent set of men, which to get together was the work of years. * * * I will continue to fill the position to which I was appointed myself; respectfully declining to follow the kind advice given."

In answer to this, on March 9th, Mr. Reid said:

NEW YORK, March 9, 1888.

SIR:

Your recent letter declining to follow the advice given in my last note, "To endeavor to reduce the expenditures to the most economical basis," is at hand.

You are hereby directed—(1) To suspend any work, if any has been begun, on any part of the third set of one hundred machines.

(2) In view of your statement that a considerable number of employees would be idle if such work were not begun, you are hereby directed to reduce the force at once to such an extent that no one shall be retained in our service who cannot be profitably employed on the work now in hand in the completion of the first and second sets of one hundred machines each. In executing this order, you will take pains, of course, to retain those operatives whose employment is most useful and economical for the company.

(3) You will report as early as practicable what reduction in the weekly pay roll can thus be effected.

(4) You will confine purchases of material for the company strictly to what is still needed for the completion of the machines of the first and second sets of one hundred each, and will report as early as possible what amount of material you think still likely to be needed for the completion of these machines. Respectfully,

[Signed] WHITELAW REID,
President and Chairman Executive Committee.

Mr. O. Mergenthaler,
    508 East Preston street,
        Baltimore, Md.

---

* The letter as given, is as quoted by Mr. Reid in a report to the Board of Directors. The omissions are his, as also in Mr. Mergenthaler's answer, dated February 28, 1888, and consist in severe strictures and criticism of Mr. Mergenthaler's management. A request for a complete copy of these letters was answered to the effect that they could not be found.

OTT. MERGENTHALER'S RESIGNATION.

BALTIMORE, March 15, 1888.

DEAR SIR:

Your orders of the 10th have come to hand. Regarding the supplies still needed for the completion of the work now on hand I estimate the same to cost about $3,500.

Regarding the reduction of the pay roll at the Camden Street Factory, I can say that within three months the same can be decreased to practically nothing; how much such decrease will amount to from week to week I am unable to tell, as the men will have to be dropped just as they get done with the work on hand.

As to the carrying into effect of the order to close the Camden Street Factory, it is with reluctance that I see myself compelled to leave the same to my successor, and herewith tender to you my resignation as Manager of the company; the same to take effect as soon as convenient, certainly, however, before the order referred to has to go into general effect. The reasons which impel me to this step are generally known to the Board and yourself, and have already formed the subject-matter of a number of communications and complaints on my part to that body or yourself as their representative.

I mention letters of May 18, 1886, March 10, 1887, April 25, 1887 (to Mr. Wm. H. Smith), November 1, 1887, November 14, 1887, and November 24, 1887.

When I was first approached on the subject of giving up my well paying machine shop and to work for the company under a salary I was not at all anxious for such a change, and finally only consented on the condition that I was to be sole manager of the shop and judge of all technical questions, a condition without which I did not see that I could successfully carry out the enterprise to which I was to be appointed.

The contract, dated November 13, 1884, was drawn up in that spirit, and contains a clause which, although in different wording, was supposed to cover that point fully.

Under this contract I have since been faithfully working for the best interests of the company, and have complied with all its provisions to the letter. Under this contract the company did get into possession of its most valuable patents which in good faith I have assigned to the company, although I am sorry to record here that on the company's part most of the provisions are still to be carried out, and that provision of my being sole manager and judge of all technical questions has never, since the advent of the Mergenthaler Company, been recognized, and was, therefore, from the start a point of contention between myself and the Board.

I leave it to the Board to decide whether the company was benefited by such disregard of the plain provisions of the contract under which I consented to render my services, but whatever may be their opinion on this point, I cannot consider any longer to hold a position for which I did not engage myself, and which I never intended to fill.

Force of circumstances, particularly the fact that a large number of worthy people have invested in this enterprise, pinning their faith in my ability to carry it to a successful end, have so far prompted me to continue in charge of a work which I had to perform under so entirely different conditions than intended and under so many needless difficulties; but now I feel that I have complied with every promise ever made by me, and that in now leaving a position which I could not fill satisfactorily to myself and the Board both I am performing but a plain duty towards myself and the company.

I leave the company (all reports to the contrary notwithstanding) as a full commercial success in a condition to economically reproduce their machines in its own factories in numbers large enough to supply the present demands, and with a staff of competent men, who, under prudent management, are able to carry on the business of the company without further direct connection with it on my part.

As to my future relations with the company, I wish to say that I will do all in my power to assist the same in any way I can, always of course provided that the company will carry out the provisions of our contract in the same good faith in which I have carried out mine.

In any work which the company may have done outside of their own shop I should like to be considered on the same basis on which others are, but I should never again, under any consideration, consent to further work under a fixed salary, or to exclusively work for any one concern and excluding all other opportunities.

In entering into the contract with the National Typographic Company it has been part consideration on my part, that by so doing it would open up an avenue for the realization of a long-cherished ambition of mine to become the head of one of the largest commercial establishments in Baltimore. The exercise of my ability as an inventor I only regarded as the route to that end.

The action of the Board in suspending work is tearing down the foundations of the structure, which to build was the result of years, and the collapse of which I cannot witness from within. I prefer to pick up the material thus thrown away and use it in the building of a new structure built upon a different basis, feeling that by doing so I can best serve the interest of the company which is bearing my name, the welfare of which I still have as much at heart as ever.

Thanking yourself and the Board of Directors for the personal deference always shown to me, and feeling extremely sorry that our official relations could not be equally harmonious as our personal ones, I remain, Yours truly,

[Signed] OTT. MERGENTHALER.

Whitelaw Reid, Esq.,
President Mergenthaler Printing Company.

So far Mr. Mergenthaler considered this matter as a mere business disagreement. He simply signified his intention of abandoning a position in which he could neither do justice to his own ability nor satisfy the expectations of his superior. He had been given to understand plainly enough that he was not thought to be the right man for the place and therefore thought that his resignation would be a welcome relief to Mr. Reid and the syndicate.

However, the letters received subsequently soon showed that Mr. Reid considered the disagreement a personal one and that he intended to punish Mr. Mergenthaler for the crime of holding views differing from his own on business matters and for the obstinacy he showed in refusing to carry out a policy with which he was not in sympathy and which in his opinion would result in plunging the enterprise into trouble and ruin.

On March 17th, 1888, a letter was received, which with the ensuing correspondence, is here given.

NEW YORK, March 17, 1888.

SIR:

Your letter of the 15th was duly received, and will be laid before the Board at its first meeting.

I beg to call your attention to the fact that my letter of the 9th inst. contained 4 specific orders, the purpose of which will be defeated by delay. Please advise me at once whether you are obeying each and all of these orders or not.   Respectfully,

Ottmar Mergenthaler, Esq.,   [Signed]   WHITELAW REID.
    508 East Preston street,
        Baltimore, Md.

BALTIMORE, March 19, 1888.

DEAR SIR:

Your letter of the 17th just at hand. In reply I should say that my answer of the 15th substantially covers all points made. I have followed orders No. 1, 3 and 4. Regarding No. 2, I thought I made myself plain; that is, I will of course not carry any employees on the pay roll who cannot be profitably employed on the work started, and a number have been dropped already. But, as appears by my former letter, I do not want to remain in my position long enough for the orders to go into general effect.

                Yours truly,
            [Signed]   OTT. MERGENTHALER.

NEW YORK, March 20, 1888.

SIR:

Your letter of the 17th inst. implies that you are not carrying out the order No. 2 in my letter of March 9th.

In view of your statement that a considerable number of employees would be idle if work were not begun on parts for a third set of 100 machines, that order directed that you should reduce the force at once to such an extent that no one should be retained in your service who cannot be profitably employed on the work now in hand in the completion of the first and second sets of 100 machines each.

You say that you do not want to remain in your position long enough for this order to go into general effect. This order was to go into effect at once. Your wishes as to future service will be laid before the Board of Directors at their meeting. Meantime, however, the object of the order is defeated by delay; and failure on your part to obey it becomes defiance of the general policy of the Directors, resulting in the waste of the company's money. It is imperative that the order should go into operation at once. A deliberate refusal to obey it could be treated only as a breach of contract, to be met by removal.

Regretting that you should drive me to the necessity, I now enquire for the last time whether you will carry into effect immediately the order No. 2 in my letter of March 9th? At the same time, I have to give notice that liabilities incurred by you in defiance of this order will be your personal liabilities, not those of the company. The fact that this week's pay roll shows practically no diminution makes this notification necessary.

                Respectfully,
            [Signed]   WHITELAW REID,
        President and Chairman Executive Committee.

O. Mergenthaler, Esq.,
    508 East Preston street,
        Baltimore, Md.

BALTIMORE, March 21, 1888.

DEAR SIR:

In answer to your communication of the 20th, please note that my letter of the 19th does not imply any such refusal as pointed out. I said plainly that I would of course not carry any employees on the pay roll which could not be profitably employed on the work now on hand. The payment has been reduced to the extent called for by your order. As to the future, an immediate acceptance of my resignation will protect the Board fully, and there ought not to be any need of removal under the circumstances.

As to the intimated breach of contract, if there is any it is on the other side. I have never consented in my contract with the company to work under direct orders such as they are made now.

Yours respectfully,

[Signed] OTT. MERGENTHALER.

Whitelaw Reid, Esq.,
President Mergenthaler Printing Company.

From the foregoing it will appear that although Mr. Mergenthaler had resigned, Mr. Reid would not accept the resignation but demanded an unconditional compliance with his orders under threat of dismissal, it will also appear that Mr. Mergenthaler had complied with all orders which in the nature of things had to go into effect immediately and had plainly stated that fact. Yet Mr. Reid insisted that he failed to carry out his orders. What Mr. Mergenthaler was contending for was to be relieved of his duties before a general suspension of work and general dismissal of employees was to take place, for the simple reason that neither money nor threats could induce him to be instrumental himself in tearing down the work which was the result of years of his best efforts and the pride of his life.

He was not working merely for wages, he was working for results. He was metaphorically speaking captain of a steamer and his plain duty to himself and others was to try to bring his ship into harbor, without regard to the course laid out for him by some of the owners. That course in his judgment led to the rocks and he was not going to risk his reputation by keeping in command until the vessel struck. All he wanted was to get off and it mattered little to him whether he was honorably relieved, discharged or thrown overboard. Under the circumstances any of the three methods named was equally honorable as far as his reputation was concerned.

Simultaneously with his resignation Mr. Mergenthaler had asked a settlement of his account with the company consisting of a claim for his tools amounting to about $6,000 and ten per cent royalty on the machines built and brought into use to date. Mr. Reid replied that the claims would be laid before the board.

On April 4th Mr. Mergenthaler's resignation was accepted and he was asked when it would be convenient for him to turn over the factories to his successor. In reply Mr. Mergenthaler suggested the propriety on the part of the company to effect a settlement of his tool claims before they asked him to turn over a property in which he still held a specific part as his own. Mr. Reid, however, immediately replied that his tool claim had no connection with his resignation and demanded an immediate surrender of the factories, which order was promptly complied with. If anything had still been wanting to convince Mr. Mergenthaler that he was singled out for punishment by Mr. Reid, the above named order supplied it. The company had now practically confiscated the tools he had brought into their establishment and gave no more assurance about a settlement than that the matter would be submitted to the board. Mr. Reid practically being the board, there could be no doubt as to the significance of this reference. Mr. Mergenthaler now found himself out of position, heavily in debt for assessments on his stock subscription, and without means of re-establishing himself in business except by the sale of his share interest in the company. All indications pointing towards an attempt by Mr. Reid to avoid liability under Mr. Mergenthaler's contract with the company, he now commenced to feel the need of legal advice and he soon engaged Mr. Chas. Marshall, of the Baltimore bar, as his attorney in both the tool claim and the royalty claim.

The expected did not wait long to materialize into certainty. In answer to a letter by Mr. Marshall, the company declined all and every responsibility under either claim, pretending that the royalty claim depended on contingencies which had not arrived and might never arrive, while in the matter of the tool claim they expressed a willingness to return the tools on proper identification, but declined to be responsible for interest, wear and tear, or loss of any sort. All of Mr. Mergenthaler's tools being incorporated with the rest of the tools and having been so used for nearly four years, identification and selection of the smaller tools was out of the question, not to speak at all of the large loss by wear and tear and the materials which of course had been used up in the service of the company years ago.

Under the circumstances Mr. Mergenthaler did not feel like attempting the impossible task of having his tools identified and extracted, and on advice of his attorney brought suit for both tools and royalty. To properly comprehend the reckless disregard of honor and obligations implied in this refusal on the part of the company it ought to be explained here that in the matter of both claims the Mergenthaler Company was clearly liable under Mr. Mergenthaler's contract with the National Typographic Company, which contract was assumed by the former company and in fact formed the whole basis of existence for the former [latter struck through, "former" written above]. Take away that contract and the Mergenthaler Company would not have had the shadow of a right for existence. However, Mr. Reid conveniently got over that point by pretending that his company assumed only the rights accruing under that instrument, but that all obligations carried with it were still to be discharged by the

National Typographic Company. Unfortunately, however, for that contention, the organic agreement under which the Mergenthaler Company had received its franchise provided in plain and specific language that the Mergenthaler Company was to discharge all liabilities of the National Typographic Company and all liabilities growing out of the conduct of the business, and was then to divide the clear profit with the latter company in equal amounts. To date, the Mergenthaler Company had actually paid all the debts and liabilities of the National Typographic Company, and Mr. Reid, in his capacity as treasurer, frequently reported to the board that he had paid such or such liabilities incurred by the National Typographic Company.

To make matters still worse for Mr. Reid's pretence, Mr. Mergenthaler held his letter, written about a year previous, in which he advises him "not to worry about the matter of his tools, as the company would do what was fair and proper in the premises"; and if anything else should be needed to emphasize the recklessness of Mr. Reid's refusal it may be found in the fact that subsequently to the above letter by Mr. Reid this same bill was referred to a committee of the National Typographic Company and by them certified to as a proper charge against that company to be discharged by the Mergenthaler Company under its contract. Putting the whole situation into a nutshell, Mr. Reid had organized the Mergenthaler Printing Company, made himself its president, bankrupted the old National Typographic Company by taking from it all valuable contracts and franchises, and now referred Mr. Mergenthaler to that company for the collection of his dues. The National Typographic Company under the existing circumstances was entirely unable to discharge any obligation of any sort whatsoever unless the Mergenthaler Printing Company should show that it had made a clear profit and declared a dividend, a contingency which at that time seemed too remote to merit serious consideration.

Dividends with large companies are, as experience shows, very much a matter of bookkeeping, and they are made or suppressed at the will of the board, often entirely independent of the real earnings. With that fact in view, Mr. Mergenthaler, under advice of his counsel, was not willing to accept the National Typographic Company as his debtor, but maintained his claims against the Mergenthaler Company and brought suit thereon without further delay. A peculiar inconsistency soon developed as to the reasons for which Mr. Reid refused to pay the royalty claim. In his letters to Mr. Mergenthaler and his attorney the objections were entirely based on technicalities as given above, while in interviews with Mr. Reid or his agents, they objected to the equity and legality of the royalty agreement, and in addition thereto Mr. Reid claimed to have been ignorant of the royalty obligation and deduced therefrom the startling conclusion that that fact invalidated Mr. Mergenthaler's right to such royalty.

Now a man may buy a piece of property believing it unencumbered and truthfully claim that he did not know of the mortgage. Yet his failure in this respect would not affect the validity of that mortgage, although ordinary business men would probably consider him a fit subject for their sympathy. But if a man organizes a company, makes himself its president and sends out printed prospectuses in which the mortgage is mentioned, then he cannot reasonably claim ignorance thereof.

The spring and early summer of 1888 passed and Mr. Mergenthaler was still without tools and without money from the company. The tool question assumed another shape almost every week, Mr. Mergenthaler several times receiving notice from the New York office that the tools were ready for delivery under some condition, only to be informed by the superintendent of the factory that he had no such orders or that his orders differed from those stated to Mr. Mergenthaler. Later, through a letter by Mr. Wm. Henry Smith, the Secretary of the company, Mr. Mergenthaler was informed that it had been decided to settle his claims and that if he would come over to New York to discuss the details there was no doubt that the matter could now be satisfactorily arranged. This was good news and unexpected at that. What could have brought about such a sudden change of sentiment? Mr. Mergenthaler hastened to New York and to his surprise found that the meeting was not to take place at Mr. Reid's office, but at some room in one of the large office buildings. The secretary of the company was there, but almost immediately on Mr. Reid entering the room he left, leaving Messrs. Reid and Mergenthaler alone by themselves.

Mr. Reid started out to say that the company had decided to settle the dispute, etc., that it would pay the tool claim in full with interest, etc., and that there should then be no further cause of contention. "Of course," he continued, "it would be of no use to settle one claim unless by so doing we can settle the other too, and all that we ask you in this respect is to give us a release of the royalty obligation." "So you ask me to abandon all my rights and all the compensation which I have to expect for my valuable invention, in return for having a bill paid which only amounts to a few thousand dollars and which I can collect through the courts, if not otherwise! No, sir, I will never do such a thing; as it is, the courts will have to settle this matter." "The courts!" Mr. Reid rejoined, "we have nothing to fear from the courts, it is an unjust contract and it is an illegal contract and courts are not very much given to enforce such contracts as that one." Mr. Reid now commenced to speak of the earnest desire of the board to arrive at an *equitable* settlement, which drew out the question by Mr. Mergenthaler what he thought an equitable settlement to be. "An equitable settlement in my opinion consists in giving you nothing, at least not on the machines used by the syndicate, but the board may think differently on that point." This was enough for Mr. Mergenthaler, and he abruptly ended the meeting, more than ever wondering about Mr. Reid's queer ways of assisting him in building castles on the Rhine.

Shortly after this meeting Mr. Mergenthaler was informed that the company had commenced the removal of the factory property to Brooklyn and he so advised his attorney. The latter at once advocated the issue of an attachment against it so as to prevent the property from being removed from the State without bond being given covering the amount of his claim. It was agreed to, but to the astonishment of everybody it was discovered that on the preceding day, Mr. Reid had sold all and every thing of the company's property in the city of Baltimore, representing a value of at least $180,000, to one Chas. R. Williams, of New York, for the ridiculously small sum of $20,000, and had made oath that the sale was a *bona fide* one and that it was made by order of the Board of Directors. Mr. Chas. R. Williams also had made oath to the fact that he was a *bona fide* purchaser. On investigation, Chas. R. Williams was found to be a man of literary pursuits, a relative of the secretary of the company, a man without financial rating by any of the mercantile agencies, and a man who never before had been in the tool business nor could have had any use for the tools and machines so bought. Considering the above facts and the further fact that the Mergenthaler Company had at least $600,000 of uncalled-for subscriptions still to collect, Mr. Mergenthaler had no difficulty in refusing to recognize this sale and of attaching the property of Chas. R. Williams for the debts of the Mergenthaler Printing Company.

Not satisfied with this remarkable transaction of selling $180,000 of property for the paltry sum of $20,000, Mr. Reid a few days after that sale leased that same property from its purchaser, had it removed at the company's expense to Brooklyn, fitted up the company's factory with it and proceeded to spend the company's money in completing the linotype machines pretended to belong to Chas. R. Williams. Finally, on January 14th, 1889, he rounded out all of the previous transactions by buying back from Chas. R. Williams all of the property included in that pretended sale for the same sum for which he had sold it, namely $20,000. As a man of accommodating habits Mr. Chas R. Williams will no doubt be fully appreciated by our readers. Himself not a man of extensive wealth, yet he is ready to help a few millionaires out of a temporary embarrassment by relieving them of the Mergenthaler Printing Company property. However, as the company needs the property so sold he leases it back, and later on, utterly blind to the big bargain he has made, he sells it back to the company without making a cent on the whole transaction which by right ought to have netted him the modest sum of at least $150,000.

THE SYNDICATE CONTRACTS WITH ITSELF FOR THE FREE USE OF THE LINOTYPE MACHINES.

Having now some idea of the standard of equity prevailing at the company's office in its dealings with Mr. Mergenthaler the reader will probably be prepared for similar dealings with other parties and we will now proceed to state how the syndicate managed to deal with the stockholders at large. We have already mentioned the damaging report of Mr. Reid in January, 1888, in regard to the result of the linotypes at the syndicate offices. It soon developed what was intended to be accomplished by it. On January 21st, 1888, shortly after Mr. Reid's statement to the stockholders, the Board of Trustees, consisting of a majority of syndicate members, voted to themselves the free use of the linotype machines for the period of one year. One month thereafter the same board struck the words "for the period of one year" from the original resolution, thus making the free use of the machines permanent. The following will give the number of free machines as voted to themselves by the syndicate: New York Tribune 30, Chicago News 20, Courier-Journal, Louisville, 18, Stilson Hutchins of the Washington Post 16, Wm. H. Rand of Rand, McNally & Co., Chicago, 20, Wm. H. Smith of 18, Clephane, Devine, White and Warburton 6. The only payment to be made for the use of these machines was $1,000 for each machine and a royalty to the company of one mill per thousand, which practically means nothing. But this was not enough, and they, in addition to the above, voted to themselves the *exclusive* use of the linotype in their respective cities, and the right to exchange any part of a machine or the whole machines free of charge for improved machines.

The full significance of the advantages thus secured to the syndicate at the expense of the general stockholders will be understood when we consider the fact that the cost of these machines to the company in actual cash was not less than $1,600 per machine and that the royalty stipulated by the stockholders was ten cents per thousand, while the syndicate paid but one mill per thousand; add to this the obligation of practically keeping the machines in repair free of charge and the right of free exchange, all of which privileges have been freely availed of, and it will be seen that the company was run for the exclusive benefit of the syndicate.

As an illustration of the real commercial value of the machines at that time we mention here the fact that in April, 1889, only fifteen months after Mr. Reid reported the machines as a heavy source of expense, that same gentleman gave a statement of the result of the machines at his composing room, from which it appears that their yearly saving amounted to over $80,000 over and above the cost of hand composition, and every other syndicate office recorded similar proportional profits to the credit of the machine.

HOW THE SYNDICATE SUCCEEDED OTHERWISE IN ADVANCING THE INTERESTS OF THE ENTERPRISE AND HOW IT IMPROVED UPON MR. MERGENTHALER'S BUSINESS METHODS

We now return to the time of Mr. Mergenthaler's resignation and note the appointment of Chas. H. Davids as his successor in charge of the factories. Mr. Davids was an elderly gentleman, well past fifty, a very fluent speaker and apparently full of energy. He had no experience in linotypes, and evidently not attaching a high value to that article, he appointed as his assistant superintendent another man who likewise was an entire stranger to the business. Mr. Davids at once made very glittering promises in regard to the great reduction of cost of manufacturing which was to be expected under his management. One of the first steps he took was to cancel all the contracts placed by Mr. Mergenthaler, reporting his action to the chairman of the executive committee, Mr. Reid. We quote Mr. Davids as follows:

"There was found to be existing in Baltimore a very loose method of having work done by contract, by which the contractor was the certain and large gainer and the company an equally certain and large loser. These leaks were all stopped, thus saving the company a large amount of money and specific reports of my action were made at the time. In some cases were found existing contracts which were nearly completed and which would have cost the company a great deal of money on their completion, but which fortunately contained clauses providing for cancellation at the company's option. No advantage had ever been taken of these provisions, but the options so conferred were immediately used to the pecuniary advantage of the company. . . . The contractor who had nearly finished the distributing rails made under contract would have gained over $1,000 above his regular salary. By taking advantage of the cancellation clause, we settled with him for the sum of $300 in full. The assembling department was run in about the same way, and on the outside contracts the terms were excessively against the company's interests. In regard to the latter I have no hesitation in saying that when our Ryerson establishment is thoroughly equipped we will be able to do the same work at a cost much less than fifty per cent of that allowed under those contracts."

Here we find Mr. Davids criticising the management of his predecessor and claiming credit for an act which really constitutes an everlasting shame to the already badly spotted name of the syndicate management. The contracts referred to contained the clause that the company should have the right to cancel them at any time before completion by paying to the contractor a certain percentage over his regular wages, and this provision was inserted for the protection of the company in case it should decide to make changes or alterations on any of the parts under contract, or in case of contractors becoming disagreeable or obstinate and thereby making themselves undesirable persons to have about the factory. In no other case was the company to take advantage of that clause and the men undertook the contracts with that specific understanding. Yet Mr. Davids cancels all contracts for the avowed purpose of confiscating the money which honest and hard-working men had earned and which belonged to them as much as his own stipulated salary belonged to him. Not only this, but he makes his action the subject of a special report to the executive, Mr. Reid, who accepts this deplorable deed without a word of censure.

As to the outside contracts, no one knew better than Mr. Mergenthaler did that the company paid rather high for them, but he had no choice in the matter, the bids were the best that could be obtained and the contracts were placed not by the free will of Mr. Mergenthaler but by order of the executive, Mr. Reid himself. About this time the company made an attempt to get the machines manufactured in their entirety by outside parties and several bids were received for their delivery, complete except as to matrices. For the result we quote Mr. Reid's report to the board, in which he says as follows: "Efforts had meantime been made to procure lower bids from responsible contractors for the construction of the entire machine, but no satisfactory bid could be had. That of the Colt Fire-Arms Company, on which the greatest hopes had been based, was for $2,200 per machine, with seven months to produce the first machine, and twenty months to deliver one hundred."

These bids constituted a most striking vindication of Mr. Mergenthaler's management, and coming almost immediately after his resignation ought to have influenced Mr. Reid to pause in his course and try to do him justice. Mr. Mergenthaler had brought out the first hundred machines in less than twenty months at a cost of only $1,300 per machine, and the progress on the second hundred gave indubitable evidence that they would be completed for $1,000 per machine, and this in spite of the fact that he had to establish a factory first before he could do any work at all, besides having the extra work of getting out the matrices, which problem in itself required fully as much time and energy as the whole balance of the machine. The lesson, however, had no such effect upon Mr. Reid; on the contrary, the more he felt the ground slipping from under his feet the more vindictive he became towards the poor inventor, as will be seen by reference to the desperate attempts he made to avoid payment of claims as just and proper as ever were made by anybody.

The next move of importance was the removal of the factory to Brooklyn, and here Mr. Davids again took occasion to emphasize his contempt for the idea that any special training was necessary on the part of the employees. He discharged the whole force of employees except a few foremen and told them that when the Brooklyn factory was equipped they might find employment again by making personal application at the new place of business, with the result that the force of experienced employees was scattered entirely, years being required before an equally efficient force was again at the disposal of the company. In the selection of the new factory building in Brooklyn the company made a decided step backwards in comparison with the places at their disposal in Baltimore, the same being small, badly lighted and the floors so low that a good-sized man could reach the ceiling with his hand.

However, the new superintendent was confident that his selection would meet all requirements and on September 10th, 1888, reported to the executive that within a year he would be able to manufacture at that place *thirty* machines per week at a cost of not over $100 per machine in wages, and that in the immediate future he would produce not less than fifteen machines per week at a cost of not more than $133 per machine. What a difference in the estimates of cost for this machine! The lowest outside bid called for $2,200 without matrices, and here is a man who after six months actual experience with it claims that he would do the same work for $100 or $135 inclusive of matrices. However, so far Mr. Davids had not completed any machines except the few left over out of the first hundred by Mr. Mergenthaler.

The syndicate too had not made contracts with anybody for the use of the machines, but instead had started to carry into practice a pet idea of Mr. Reid, consisting in the establishing of a composing room on the company's own account for the purpose of educating operators, a scheme which was doomed to fail before it was commenced. Accordingly one floor of the new factory was reserved for the reception of the machines, and as fast as they were completed they were now ushered into this composing room and operators put to work to learn the intricacies of the new way of typesetting. If the company ever expected to derive any advantage from the operators educated at its expense, the material ought to have been drawn from the most competent of hand compositors, for the reason that in justice to the machines it could ill afford to send medium or low grade men should any office ask for the services of the company's operators. To get such men, the company would have had to offer good wages and the assurance of easily securing permanent employment on the machines at the offices of some of the prospective users of the machine. The syndicate, however, had not only stopped taking orders, but had decreed that no machines should be used in New York, Chicago, Louisville, and Washington. What inducement was there then for the compositors of those cities to undergo the trouble of learning the linotype if by so doing they only reduced their pay without increasing their chances for regular employment?

As might be expected under these conditions, the company's composing room attracted not the flower of the compositor's craft, but the man who could not make good wages on regular composition, the man who is habitually out of work, the jack of all trades, and last but not least, the lady typewriter, from which class at least fifty per cent of the operators were drawn. Considering the fact that no newspaper of any consequence ever employed female compositors with satisfactory results, it is hard to see what was expected from this class of learners. The same reasons which made the female compositor an undesirable employee on hand work, would naturally work against her as a machine operator in an even more pronounced way. Assuming therefore all other conditions to be favorable, the scheme would have been doomed on account of the material selected for operators.

But there existed other drawbacks not less formidable than those mentioned. Mr. Reid attempted to do bookwork on the machines at the company's office while he himself at his own composing room had difficulties in maintaining the machines in a condition to do even medium class newspaper work. He started his learners on the task of accomplishing that which was impossible, and the result of it was discouragement and despair instead of confidence in himself and his machine on the part of the operator. Add to the foregoing the slovenly way in which the machines were erected, and the reader familiar with composing rooms can draw for himself a picture of this model establishment on the company's own premises. Imagine some forty machines in a room not over eight feet high, packed so closely that passage between them became difficult, the gas pipes leaking, the smoke pipes dripping, the poisonous vapors escaping at every joint and every outlet. Add to this the hissing of forty air blasts and Bunsen burners, the rattle of the matrices and the noise of forty pumps and clutches, and then picture forty excited learners frantically trying to make living wages against the heavy odds that were against them, and you have a fair picture of what the company called its composing room. A sawmill was noiseless in comparison, a dry kiln not so hot, a gas factory contained purer air, and the stock exchange on Black Friday could show no more excitement than was here displayed by the unfortunate operators and the still more unfortunate machinists in charge.

The success the company met with in the conduct of its composing room may be best judged by quoting from Mr. Reid's yearly report of January, 1889. In it he says: " It has already earned $700.00 or $800.00 on composition of books and pamphlets. . . . It was compelled to decline several books offered before the holidays on account of lack of operators. It now has seven operators who are paid a very moderate price for corrected work and seventeen learners who are paid nothing. . . . It is believed, however, that the job office ought to be made not only self-sustaining, but a source of considerable direct profit, while indirectly its advantages will be incalculable in furnishing a school for operators and a supply from which they can be drawn for other establishments seeking to introduce the machines." If this composing room had ever earned the cost of the gas burned in it, not to speak of wages, supervision, and other incidental expenses, we never heard of the fact.

Mr. Davids in the meantime was trying hard to redeem his promises as to cheap machines and the following statement will give an idea of the amount of success attending his efforts. When Mr. Mergenthaler retired early in April, 1888, he had practically completed the first hundred machines and the parts for a second hundred were nearly completed. In January, 1889, there were completed all told 140 machines exclusive of the first twelve, thus giving Mr. Davids credit for the assembling of forty machines and the completion of the few parts which he still found wanting. His expenses for wages alone amounted as near as can be calculated to $33,325, thus calling for an expenditure of $833 per machine, not for the making but only for assembling them, and finishing a small number of parts. A committee afterwards appointed to determine the cost of the second lot of one hundred machines found that their cost amounted to about $2,500, whereas under Mr. Mergenthaler's management these same machines would have been delivered at a cost not exceeding $1,000, a very sad showing indeed for the man who promised to produce complete machines for $133 in wages or about $180 inclusive of material.

THE DESIGN OF THE PRESENT MACHINE.

Having chronicled the business success of the syndicate management we will return to the time of Mr. Mergenthaler's resignation and follow his actions during the eventful and trying days of the quarrel with Mr. Reid. We have already learned that he left the company with the latter in possession of his tools and machinery and also of the money due him on accrued royalties. Worse than that, he was in debt to Mr. Reid for advanced money on assessments amounting to nearly $9,000, for which the latter held his overdue note. Outside of his stock in the Mergenthaler and National Typographic Company he had no assets to fall back on. It is true, he owned the dwelling he lived in, but this was subject to a mortgage and nobody buys anything without discovering such encumbrances, Mr. Reid of course excepted. Subject to the mortgage the house would not have produced anything worth mentioning. Yet he was confronted with the task of re-establishing himself in business and money had to be raised in some way.

The only way left for him was to dispose of part of his stock and he did so, by selling one-half of his holdings in each company at a price already much lower than could have been obtained four months previous. Mr. Reid's note was taken up first and the balance was used in the first payment on a factory property which he had bought. The place had been destroyed by fire and had to be rebuilt at a cost of about $7,000. The contract for this work was given out, and Mr. Mergenthaler now felt that pending the erection and equipment of this place he had time to devote himself to the improvement of the existing linotype machine. He had secured the services of Mr. Alfred Peterson, a very able draughtsman, to assist him in the new design and the work thereon was commenced within a few weeks after leaving the company's services. The Tribune machine was an undoubted commercial success, but it was not the best that could be made. Experience had shown quite a number of weak points, yet, as stated before, the wise managers of the syndicate had served an injunction on him against making any changes or improvements. He was now free and determined to make another effort to improve the machine in every way possible, the more so because he had already realized the fact that commercially the syndicate had nearly killed the prospects of the 1886 machine by their damaging report, and would certainly complete the job by the establishment of its composing room and the utter confusion and demoralization which would follow the removal of the factory to Brooklyn.

The 1886 machine required an air blast for propelling the matrices and for heating the gas, which was found to be very noisy and objectionable in a number of ways. The keyboard touch was hard and not uniform, it took some practice to operate the keyboard without causing matrices to fly out of the channel, the locking up and alignment features were rather unreliable, the distributor was not as strong as it could be, and the machine as a whole lacked that ease of accessibility which is so necessary to keep machines in their proper condition. Another drawback was the fact that each set of matrices had to have its special set of channels, a condition which was found to be quite objectionable in the manufacture of the machine, for the reason that machines could not be finished at random like now, but had to await the order of the future user as to the font of matrices he wanted to run in the machine.

In all these particulars Mr. Mergenthaler now attempted to improve, besides making the machine still faster and better suited to the higher class of composition, such as books and periodicals. We leave it to the reader to judge how near he has solved the problem then before him.

Engaged in this work months passed and the settlement of the financial question with the company appeared more remote every day. A small fraction of his tools were returned when the company removed its shops to Brooklyn, but money could not be had. His new factory building neared completion and had to be paid for, but there was no chance of getting it out of the company. The courts were not in session and his lawyer claimed that he was powerless to expedite payment of the claims. The summer passed and fall made its appearance and still the company was obstinate. In the meantime one hundred shares of stock after another had passed into the broker's hands to be sold to defray necessary expenses, until by January, 1889, he had practically sacrificed his whole interest in both companies. As a matter of course, the stock was declining continuously and the last lot sold did not realize the amount of the assessment which had been paid on them.

In the late fall of 1888 Mr. Mergenthaler, weakened by years of overwork and the extra tribulations brought about by Mr. Reid's unjust and vindictive course towards him, fell an easy victim to a serious attack of pleurisy which came very near ending his life, but from which he recovered after a hard struggle of nearly two months. After his convalescence the physicians expressed the fear that the attack might have laid the foundation for that worst of all diseases, consumption, an apprehension which later developments proved to have been only too well-founded.

Towards the close of the year Mr. Mergenthaler had completed the plans for the machine of to-day and he so informed his Washington friends, stating at the same time that his financial condition would not allow him to commence actual work in carrying the design into practice. Like many times before, it again remained for that enthusiastic and resourceful friend of the machine, Mr. J. O. Clephane, to furnish the means and thus avoid delay in a matter on which the whole future of the enterprise seemed now to depend. He at once made a visit to the more prominent shareholders in Washington and on the next day returned to Baltimore with ten contributions of $200 each in the shape of a loan to Mr. Mergenthaler for the purpose of enabling him to start the building of his improved linotype on condition that he should refund the money whenever the company would take up the construction of the machine and pay him for work done on it.

By this time the Washington stockholders had become thoroughly aroused to the mischief done by the syndicate management during the last year. The syndicate contract with themselves, the unjustifiable treatment of Mr. Mergenthaler, their failure to place machines into any office except their own and the total destruction of the manufacturing facilities had had their effect upon these stockholders and they were seriously considering the question of bringing about a change of management.

This endeavor resulted in the formation of a pool for the purpose of taking the control from the syndicate management and keeping the same for the next three years. While apparently inimical to the syndicate, yet considering all the existing conditions it will be found that the formation of this combination was carried on with the full approval of the syndicate members as furnishing them a welcome opportunity to slip out and leave it to their successors to extricate the company from the deplorable difficulties into which they had plunged it. Had the syndicate really opposed this movement it would have been a very easy matter for them to go into the market and secure an actual majority of the stock, the price of which had fallen away below the amount of assessments paid thereon and which was offered in large quantities with no one to take it. Had the syndicate refused to yield control they would have had to face the results of their recklessness and doubtful transactions, while Mr. Reid would have been compelled to either recede from the position he had assumed towards Mr. Mergenthaler or else explain before the courts that famous *bona fide* sale of the company's property which we have spoken of heretofore, an alternative in which the one course was probably as repugnant to him as the other. By yielding the control, however, both dilemmas could be avoided, which may explain the inaction of the syndicate in the matter of opposing the formation of the pool.

The pool was successful, and in January, 1889, it selected a new board, Hon. L. G. Hine again being chosen President and General Manager. Mr. Reid in his yearly report gave the machine a parting kick by stating that the machines had developed so many defects that it was thought best to discontinue all work on the third lot of machines and confine efforts exclusively to the completion of the machines still left unfinished out of the second hundred. Indeed a worthless machine it must have been if we consider the fact that less than three months later this same gentleman made a statement for publication, from which it appeared that at that time the Tribune was saving $1,600 per week over hand composition by the use of thirty-three machines, or over $80,000 per year, and that too without any improvements having been applied to the machines in question between the respective dates of the two statements.

THE MANAGEMENT UNDER HON. L. G. HINE'S LEADERSHIP.

The new management on entering upon its duties found itself face to face with a most difficult and trying situation. The reputation of the machines had been ruined, not a single order was on hand, the efficiency of the factory had been destroyed, a very costly composing room had been fastened upon the company which instead of aiding in the sale of machines really constituted the strongest argument against their use, New York, Philadelphia, Washington, Chicago, and Louisville were excluded as a possible field for the machines, and the relations of the company to the inventor and originator of the whole enterprise were in a condition of complete rupture.

One of the first acts done by the new board was to order the assumption of work on the improved machine to be carried on by Mr. Mergenthaler and to give him such assurance of the good will of the new management as would secure his hearty co-operation in the interest of the company. A committee was appointed to investigate the syndicate management, a new superintendent of manufacturing was appointed, and an earnest effort made to obtain orders for machines. This last named point indeed was not an easy task, and if it resulted in but very limited success it was indeed not because of insufficiency of effort. Every report so far given out by Mr. Reid as president of the company was detrimental to the machine, and without some positive acknowledgment of the merits of the machine by the syndicate officers every effort in that direction was useless. Mr. Reid and his colleagues were prevailed upon to furnish statements of the actual results obtained at their offices and they finally consented.

These statements showed that the syndicate was using the machines with enormous profit to themselves, and Mr. Hine and his co-workers took pains to give the widest possible circulation to the figures thus obtained, yet the result was disappointment, as might well have been expected. The publishers were now confronted with three reports by Mr. Reid, two of them as president of the company to the stockholders, decidedly detrimental to the machine, and one, following but three months later, which was as favorable to it as the former were unfavorable. Assuming that the president of a company would report nothing to the stockholders except the actual facts and knowing that the last statement was published with the purpose of advertising the machine to the public, it may well be imagined that even the extremely favorable state of affairs disclosed by these reports failed entirely in their purpose to induce others to use the machine. The syndicate officers too were prevailed upon to accept a modification of the exclusion of the large cities as a field for the machines, but without result; the machine had been made unsalable, and but for the special efforts of Mr. Abner Greenleaf, who succeeded in getting an order for twelve machines from the Providence Journal, not a single machine would have been placed in this country.

The most delicate point of all to deal with was the composing room. Carrying it on as it was, ruined the reputation of the machines, and abandoning it would be construed as a confession of inability on the part of the company to use the machines profitably in its business and thus result in the same end. Mr. Mergenthaler seeing the utter hopelessness of the attempt to do bookwork with a machine not adapted for it, at once advocated the closing of the composing room, but Mr. Hine insisted on making an effort to render this department more efficient and make it at least self-sustaining. However, the task was too great and finally it had to be abandoned.

In the meantime a branch company had been organized in England and some sixty of these machines were sold to that company for $1,000 per machine, the rest of them after considerable delay were placed into a New York office on a royalty agreement, but as they were mostly used on book and job work they were out of their natural sphere of usefulness and never returned anything worth mentioning to the company. Thus ended the first two hundred machines built by the company. The company expended on them in the neighborhood of $380,000 and received for them about $160,000, and yet, without the manipulations of the syndicate, these same machines should and would have returned to the company a yearly revenue of at least $300 per machine, or $60,000 per year, more than enough to pay six per cent interest on all the money actually expended upon the enterprise up to that time.

THE MISTAKE OF HIS LIFE.

How Mr. Mergenthaler was Induced to Accept $50 Instead of Ten Per Cent of Cost on Each Machine.

Another matter to which the new management applied itself was the regulation of the relations existing between the inventor, Mr. Mergenthaler, and the Mergenthaler Printing Company. While the latter in its original agreement with the National Typographic Company assumed all liabilities of the National Typographic Company, yet no direct agreement between the inventor and the Mergenthaler Printing Company was existing, and as we have learned before, Mr. Whitelaw Reid opposed Mr. Mergenthaler's claim with all the cunning and vehemence at his command.

The Washington stockholders had now taken up Mr. Reid's cry of "too much royalty" and a committee was appointed to see whether a modification of the original agreement could not be effected with Mr. Mergenthaler. The committee consisted of three of the most intimate friends of Mr. Mergenthaler, men who enjoyed his confidence and therefore were most excellently suited for the work entrusted to them, and they succeeded in doing what Mr. Reid could never have accomplished with his high-handed way of disregarding existing agreements and repudiating the company's obligation under the royalty contract. They did not deny the company's liability, but based their case entirely on the expediency of Mr. Mergenthaler accepting a reduction of royalty in order to re-establish good feeling within the company and induce new faith in the future of the enterprise.

They pointed out to him, that whatever was the underlying cause, the fact remained that so far the enterprise had resulted disastrously to the stockholders and that the prospect before them was still nothing better than a long period of assessments with no show of dividends in the near future. Mr. Reid by his agitation on the subject had so badly scared the stockholders about the ruinous effect of the ten per cent royalty to the inventor that the interests of all concerned demanded that something should be done to re-establish confidence in the future prospects of the company, and they offered a royalty of $50 per machine, which amounted to a reduction of over one-half of the royalty payable under the ten per cent clause. It was not the intention of the company, they explained, to actually reduce the prospective profits to the inventor, but only to put them into a shape in which they could not be used in future for the purpose of discrediting the prospects of the company, and in return for Mr. Mergenthaler's concession they promised that he would be favored otherwise in the line of contracts for the company and increased influence within it.

As Mr. Hine expressed himself, "If Mr. Mergenthaler will consent to this modification he will so endear himself to the company and the stockholders at large that no request of his could be refused, and his position within the company will become impregnable for all time to come, the indirect advantages of which will be worth more to him in dollars and cents than the money he will give up under the proposed agreement."

Mr. Mergenthaler yielded, and here he made the mistake of his life. Promises made by a company are only made to be broken, at least they will not last any longer than the term of office of those who made them, and such was the case here. He received contracts for machines, but only so long as he could furnish them cheaper than the company could build them at their own shops. He was allowed a fair influence within the company, but only so long as Mr. Hine remained its president. Other favors of any sort were neither asked nor received under Mr. Hine's management, and after the Reid party again assumed power there were not only no favors for the inventor, but ordinary justice was denied in almost every case and every means employed to avoid paying even the insignificant sum left as his compensation under that agreement, while in the matter of influence, that was reduced to the zero point.

Not only that, he found no encouragement in his efforts to still further improve the machine, but on the contrary he had to make improvements at his own expense and against their protest. The column base, including improvements on justifying and locking devices, the present excellent keyboard, the duplex arrangement, the channel plate with hinged ends, the double e and n channel, the two line letter, and many other little improvements made between 1891 and 1895, were nearly all made at Mr. Mergenthaler's expense, and it took years in some cases before the company could be induced to embody them in the machines made in their own factory. We have here the peculiar spectacle of a company constantly being opposed to its own best interest and yet finally getting into possession of an excellent machine, not as a consequence of proper and wise measures on its own part, but in spite of itself and its own acts.

In the meantime Mr. Mergenthaler had well advanced the construction of the improved machine, and in 1889 brought the same to a trial which showed this machine to be an unqualified success and far superior to the existing machines in speed, quality of work and general substantiality. However, it was entirely too heavy, a fault brought about by the draughtsman's general inclination from which he could hardly ever free himself entirely. It was therefore decided to lighten the patterns as much as possible and to build from them a second machine which was to serve as the pattern for large numbers to be built thereafter. This second machine was finished in February, 1890, and soon thereafter exhibited at the Judge Building in New York under the direction of those long-tried friends of the machine and its inventor, Messrs. J. O. Clephane and Abner Greenleaf.

The exhibition was a success in the full sense of the word and resulted in orders for several hundreds of machines within a period of a few months. At last the prejudice of the printing trade had been overcome and there was no longer any difficulty in leasing machines to newspaper men. The 1888 machine, according to published statements, was a great money saver, and here was another machine twice as fast, capable of doing better work and requiring neither air-blast nor electricity. In view of these great advantages it was decided to increase the yearly lease on each machine from $300 (the lease price of the 1886 machine) to $500 for the new machine, and yet the new machine could be easily placed at that price while nobody could be induced to hire the old machines at $200 less. It will be noticed that the company was by no means a loser through the substitution of the improved machine for the original one, but not so the inventor. He had made a machine doing twice the amount of work and had allowed his royalty to be reduced over fifty per cent, which in practice amounted to an actual reduction of over seventy-five per cent of the amount originally stipulated. For every two machines formerly, there was but one required now, hence the inventor's royalty would suffer to the same extent. In return, he had the promise of being kept indirectly harmless and of having secured the everlasting obligation of the stockholders, which promise as time rolled on finally vanished into thin air and nothingness.

While Mr. Mergenthaler was engaged in building the machine later exhibited at the Judge Building, the Brooklyn works of the company, under Mr. W. Scudder, were kept busy on a lot of twelve machines made from the same patterns and designs furnished by Mr. Mergenthaler and used in his works. It soon developed that in the company's own works the same difficulties would have to be gone through again in the manufacture of the improved machine as had been experienced in Baltimore in the first attempts to manufacture the old machine. There were no special tools for the new construction, and when the parts were made and ready for assembling they would not satisfactorily assemble. The superintendent no

THE LINOTYPE MACHINE.
(Improved Model 1, exhibited at the Judge Building in 1890)

doubt worked hard and tried his best, but completed machines would not materialize. Mr. Mergenthaler himself made several trips to Brooklyn to help matters along and finally sent two of his best men who had worked on the Judge Building machine to assist in making machines out of the individual parts. After a great deal of delay they were finally finished and in October, 1890, placed in the composing room of the Brooklyn Standard Union as the first machines of the improved type entering into commercial use.

The installation of the machines at this office was of particular significance not so much because of its size and standing as a newspaper, but because of the fact that it was an office belonging under the jurisdiction of the Typographical Union. It meant that the powerful resistance which the Union had so far offered to the machines had been overcome and that henceforth there would be no obstacle to placing linotype machines in other Union offices. It amounted to a concession on the part of the Union that the merits of the machine made it irresistible, and it was mainly due to the untiring efforts of Mr. Hine, the president of the company, that the members of the Union were given proper attention and that full opportunity was afforded them to investigate the capabilities of the machine before they were asked to accept it and establish a scale of wages under which it would be tolerated in their offices. The first results obtained at the Standard Union were hardly satisfactory, mainly due to the fact that the machines showed many points of weakness, due to defective workmanship and inexperience of those who handled them, not excepting the machinists, yes, even the superintendent of the factory himself. Yet, after a while, the existing difficulties were corrected, thus giving the operators a fair chance to show what they and the machines were capable of.

In honor to the men first employed on these machines it must be said that every one of them soon made a first class record for himself and most of them were heard of later on from different other offices as record breakers on linotype composition. All of these men were taken from the regular employees at the Standard Union, and not from the former graduates of the company's composing room, as the reader probably would expect. There was no opening for the latter on any of the newspapers equipped with linotypes from the fact that every newspaper showed sufficient consideration for their old employees to desire that they should have the first opportunity on the linotype, and from our observation in this respect we think we are safe to say that there is not a single newspaper within the United States which would at that time have been willing to discharge its old employees and employ in their place a set of even the most experienced linotype operators even if they could have been furnished for the asking.

So far the invention had been free from imitators and infringements, but "it is a bad thing which does not find infringers." In conformity with this rule, at about the time of the first use of the improved machines at the Standard Union, a bold and well organized attempt was made to introduce into the market a comparatively ineffective machine, a bold and barefaced imitation of the linotype, called the Rogers Typograph.

This machine had but half of the capacity of the linotype and was its inferior in nearly every other respect, but being considerably smaller in size and being advertised with as much energy and hornblowing as Barnum's Circus or Higgins German Laundry Soap, it looked for awhile as if it would conquer the field before the linotype interests could carry their case into court and get a decision for infringement against this pirate. Several of these machines had been placed in the composing room of the New York World, and with the assistance of G. W. Turner, business manager of the World and also financially interested in the Rogers machine, as much capital was made for the new interloper as the case would permit. However, the kite did not fly very long. The Mergenthaler Company, led by its president, at once brought suit for a temporary injunction. Their case was entrusted to the well known law firm of Betts, Atterbury, Hyde and Betts of New York, under whose able management, assisted by Mr. Hine's untiring energy and experience, a well deserved and quick victory was won over the opposing forces by the issue of a preliminary injunction against the Rogers Typograph on March 11th, 1891, which injunction was sustained and made permanent later, the final appeal of the Rogers Typograph Company being decided against them in December, 1894.

With this matter out of the way we return to the company's efforts to get its own machine upon the market. In April, 1890, a contract had been given to the inventor for the construction of one hundred machines at a cost of $1,200 per machine, all complete except matrices and spaces, an equal number was started at the company's works in Brooklyn and work was pushed in both establishments with all energy possible.

It was expected at that time to commence delivering machines out of this order as early as October, but it took up to January, 1891, before the first one of them was finished by Mr. Mergenthaler under his contract, and the Brooklyn factory could not commence delivery before February, 1891. In April, 1891, the New Orleans Times-Democrat was equipped with machines from the Baltimore factory, and this paper was followed quickly by installations at the Cincinnati Commercial, the Montgomery Advertiser, the Atlanta Constitution and others, while the Brooklyn works equipped the office of the Canadian Government at Ottawa, the Troy Press, Commercial Bulletin, New York, Albany Journal and others.

The time and money which had to be expended toward the production of special tools for these machines were found to be a far more serious matter than was expected and resulted in great delay and high cost at both the Brooklyn and Baltimore factories. Mr. Mergenthaler soon discovered that he would lose money under his contract, but his energy and the special advantages he had as the inventor and maker of the first machines let him off with a comparatively small loss, while the cost of the machines made at the company's own works ran up to at least two thousand dollars. As was the case before under Mr. Reid's management in 1888 so it happened again in this case. The delay and greater cost of production were attributed to the improvements, corrections and additional measures which Mr. Mergenthaler made as time rolled on and more experience was gained from the working of the machines then in practical operation. Mr. Hine, who as a rule knew how to appreciate improvements, now became impatient and on February 9th, 1891, issued the following order to the superintendent of the Brooklyn factory:

W. S. SCUDDER, ESQ., Supt. of Manufacturing.

You will complete the linotypes now under construction at the factory strictly like the standard machine just tested and not permit any change therefrom nor deviation without my written approval or a written statement of its necessity. You will not permit any experimental work or any work not essential to complete these machines nor furnish supplies to complete machines without my written order.

A similar order was sent to Mr. Mergenthaler and the order printed and sent to the stockholders, together with the explanation that on account of the many and continuous changes made by Mr. Mergenthaler in the working drawings the Brooklyn factory had made but slow progress, hence this order was deemed necessary. At the same time this circular claims that since this order has been in force the Brooklyn factory had made more apparent progress. In explanation of the above we will say that as a matter of course Mr. Mergenthaler was always anxious to get the machine into the highest state of perfection and also reduce its cost wherever possible, and to that end believed in making immediate use of anything experience showed to be of advantage. The changes he made in the working drawings, far from being a hindrance to the speedy completion of the machines, materially aided towards that end, and in nearly all cases implied a saving of time and cost, yet the Brooklyn factory had to have an excuse for the delay and the superintendent seized the opportunity to get one that was plausible.

The deplorable result of this order soon showed itself. No more changes were made in Brooklyn, but Mr. Mergenthaler, in spite of the order, continued to carefully note every point, and immediately applied any improvement or simplification he could think of on the machines still uncompleted out of his first contract, with the result that when he had delivered the last machine out of this first contract their average cost was found to be a little over $1,100 per machine, while the Brooklyn machines had cost over $2,000. Besides this great difference in cost, Mr. Mergenthaler's machines always represented the state of the art at the time the machines were made, while those made by the company represented the state of the art as it was six months or a year before. When Mr. Mergenthaler delivered his last machine under that contract it was a neat and smooth working machine, while the last machine out of the first hundred made by the company itself was as rough in looks and as jerky and noisy in action as the very first ones that had left the factory.

They now were ready to adopt Mr. Mergenthaler's improvements for use in the next lot of one hundred machines and so it has kept on to this very date. What an idea, to store up the experience gained in one lot for exclusive use in the next! Why not make use of your experience at once? What would Mr. Hine and what would his successor say of the incipient lawyer who after leaving the Law School should resolve to run his first one hundred cases exclusively on the experience and knowledge of the law he had gained when he passed his examination, and reserve all experience and additional knowledge of law acquired in the prosecution of these cases for exclusive use in his second batch of one hundred cases? True, the lawyer would probably dispose of his cases with less trouble to himself, but where does his client come in? And how about the lawyer's reputation? Yet this rule if applied to law practice is the same as when applied to the conduct of a manufacturing business, and its effects are no more absurd and disastrous in one case than in the other.

Under Mr. Hine's successor the resistance against anything in the line of improvements was even more pronounced than before and hundreds of machines were made with the old box base, old keyboard, weight actuated justification levers, old noisy clutch mechanism and other shortcomings, long after Mr. Mergenthaler had improved the construction of these parts and applied the improvements on the machines made at his factory, with the result that the users of the machine are compelled to battle with the disadvantages of an antiquated construction for years until they finally succeed in having the company make the changes either free of charge or at a mere nominal cost.

Thus the customer has to suffer by using an old construction and the company in no way escapes the trouble of making the change, it only delays making that change and for its penalty has to pay the cost of the change, which is far greater if made at the customer's composing room than it would be at the company's factory.

Towards the fall of 1891 new difficulties commenced to threaten the company in the form of an exhaustion of its treasury funds. Nearly two hundred machines had been completed and placed in commission, but the royalty derived therefrom was entirely insufficient to meet the heavy expenses of producing more machines. This state of affairs resulted in the reorganization of the enterprise and a consolidation of the Mergenthaler and National Typographic Companies, under the name of the Mergenthaler Linotype Company of New Jersey, with a capital stock of $5,000,000, three millions of which were equally divided between the stockholders of the Mergenthaler Printing Company and those of the National Typographic Company, while the remaining two millions were placed into the treasury to be sold to provide further capital with which to continue the manufacture of more machines.

The transaction therefore amounted to watering the stock to the extent of three additional shares to every two existing before. One million of the new stock was soon thereafter sold to a syndicate, consisting of D. O. Mills, Ogden Mills, W. C. Whitney and others, for about one-third of its face value, and with this transaction the control of the company again passed out of the hands of the Washington stockholders and into practically the same hands which four years previous had caused so much disturbance within the company. The Messrs. Mills being respectively the father-in-law and brother-in-law of Mr. Whitelaw Reid, it is perhaps not to be wondered at if from now on we now and then find distinct traces of the same spirit of injustice and ill will towards Mr. Mergenthaler which characterized the early dealing of that gentleman with the inventor.

Mr. Hine in December, 1891, left the services of the company, and Mr. Phil. T. Dodge of Washington, D. C., was elected in his place.

MR. DODGE'S MANAGEMENT.

The task which Mr. Dodge had to assume on entering upon his duties was a comparatively easy one. He started with two factories at his command, both equipped for the work and unhampered by the thousands of difficulties and delays incident to the initial stages of a manufacturing establishment. He assumed an established business with the resistance of the Typographical Union and of the publishers overcome, one hundred and sixty machines of the new kind in actual successful operation, with fifty-two more either in transit for delivery or ready for delivery at the factories. In addition to this, he found another lot of 100 machines nearly completed at the Brooklyn works, and a newly replenished treasury of $374,000, with a yearly revenue from the already existing machines amounting actually to $80,000, and which could be rapidly augumented by delivery of more machines which from that time on were assured to be made with regularity.

One of his first official acts was to ask Mr. Mergenthaler for a full statement of all the obligations of the company to him. This statement was furnished and amongst other items contained a charge of some $1,300 for patent drawings and for designing the last machine, which had already proven such an enormous commercial success for the company. The bill in question was for the work done by Mr. Mergenthaler, his draughtsman and a patent draughtsman after he left the employment of the company in 1888; over one-half of it represented cash paid to the draughtsman and the rest represented Mr. Mergenthaler's own time for the period between April and December, 1888, when the Washington stockholders furnished two thousand dollars to carry on the construction work.

During the period covered by the bill Mr. Mergenthaler received neither a salary nor royalty from the company and the bill in every respect was as just and proper a charge as any ever made against the company. It had not been presented before for the reason that the charge stood on the books as a charge against Mr. Mergenthaler, there being no order for this work from the company for reasons well known to Mr. Dodge. A change of clerks having taken place between the time this work was done and the time the company assumed responsibility for it, the new clerk failed to discover this old charge, hence the failure to attempt collection before. These matters were all explained to Mr. Dodge and there was not the shadow of a doubt in Mr. Mergenthaler's mind that the bill representing so much merit and equity would be paid at once and with pleasure.

Had not the work charged under this bill already resulted in giving the company a yearly income of $100,000? Were there not millions in immediate sight as its direct result? And would not the company have lost at least eight months of time, had Mr. Mergenthaler not used his time and money in the interest of the company at a time when the latter in a blind frenzy tried to ruin him financially?

Nobody knew these facts better than Mr. Dodge did, yet, to Mr. Mergenthaler's indescribable surprise and disgust, that gentleman in a very smooth and courteous letter calmly explained that he did not see his way clear to pass the bill in question, not because he doubted the correctness of the bill, not because he failed to see the equity of the bill, no, but simply for the reason "that it was not a legal charge against the Company." The company had never given an order for the work done under it, and hence probably Mr. Dodge's conclusion as to lack of legality. Mr. Mergenthaler's reply was to the effect that he did not present the bill in question as a legal charge against his company but as one full of merit and equity. He maintained the equity of the claim against the company and presented the bill once or twice every year. Finally in 1896, when the company had already made millions out of the enterprise, Mr. Dodge offered to pay one-half of the amount. Mr. Mergenthaler, however, insisted on either collecting the whole bill or nothing at all and finally the bill was paid as it stood.

The reader would probably, from the action of Mr. Dodge, conclude the existence of strained relations between the inventor and the new president, but such was not the case, the personal relations between them at the commencement of Mr. Dodge's term being absolutely friendly and Mr. Mergenthaler's devotion to the interests of the company unquestioned and unquestionable. It was simply one of Mr. Dodge's peculiar ways to intensify the inventor's devotion to the interests of the company and probably akin to Mr. Reid's peculiarities regarding the protection of the inventor's interest.

The next thing attracting the new president's attention was the cost of maintaining the two hundred machines now out on rental in proper repair. These machines had all been placed in commission during the last six months and as a matter of course were served by inexperienced operators and machinists, and the natural results of the situation were many breakages and heavy repair bills to which many of the offices objected.

Mr. Dodge, seriously alarmed about this condition of affairs, wrote one letter of complaint after another to the inventor picturing the situation in the darkest possible colors and predicting the complete financial failure of the enterprise unless the repair charges could be reduced at once, making at the same time all kinds of impracticable suggestions for changes in the machines. Mr. Mergenthaler's reply was to the effect that no material changes were necessary, that the many breakages were mostly due to the inexperience of the operators and machinists, and that no matter what changes would be made, a linotype could never be made so strong that inexperienced men could not cause damage. At the same time Mr. Mergenthaler called his attention to the several improvements he had already introduced into his machines which would to some extent reduce the possibility of accidental breakage. The best, however, the company could do just now was to reduce the cost of maintenance of machines to the customers by a reasonable reduction of the price list for repair parts, which at the time called for profits amounting on many parts to four hundred per cent.

Here we have a condition of things which, in the president's own opinion, was ruinous to the future prospects of the enterprise and which therefore should have required immediate action. Yet, with characteristic indecision, the new president neither adopts the improvements suggested by the inventor nor does he reduce the cost of repair parts, but calmly continues to bombard the inventor with letters of complaint and keeps on collecting an average of at least three hundred per cent profit on the repair parts, thus maintaining the very conditions which he claimed would prevent the introduction of machines in other offices, a condition for which there was not the slightest excuse. It took years before he consented to reduce the cost of repair parts, and when it finally was done, the real need of it had passed, for there were then out thousands of machines with hundreds of orders on hand,

and the frequency of breakage had been greatly reduced as predicted by Mr. Mergenthaler.

A new and quite unexpected move against the interests of the company was inaugurated shortly after Mr. Hine left the services of the company, and for a while it looked as if the matter might become a very serious impediment to its future prospects. Mr. Scudder, the superintendent of the Brooklyn factory, claimed to have invented a machine called the monoline, which was to be far superior to the linotype in point of simplicity and cheapness and as efficient as the linotype in every respect. It soon developed too that he had made arrangements with Mr. Hine for the purpose of developing the machine. With this act the superintendent had identified himself with an interest squarely opposed to the one he was supposed to serve, and under generally recognized business principles he ought to have been relieved from his post at once. The position he held required the full and undivided efforts of its incumbent and it was necessary that he should serve the company not only with his hands, but with the whole man, hands, brain, heart and everything. Yet Mr. Dodge allowed him to continue in charge for six months and until he finally abandoned his place voluntarily. It is not our intention to discredit Mr. Scudder in any way, form or manner, but only to point out the fact that no ordinary man is ever able to render efficient services to anybody with his monetary interests opposed to the interests of his employer, and that in allowing this man to continue in charge of the company's manufacturing establishment Mr. Dodge engaged in an experiment with all the chances of success against the company.

In June, 1892, Mr. Scudder resigned his position and the general manager was now compelled to face the all-important question of making a proper selection of a new superintendent for the company's manufacturing establishment. The position required a man thoroughly familiar with the specialty the company was engaged in; no other, no matter how bright, how energetic and how well versed in general mechanics, could ever be expected to render efficient services without undergoing first the costly and slow process of acquiring a complete knowledge of the machine, which in the case of so complicated a contrivance as the linotype must be a matter of many months if not years.

As was customary for Mr. Dodge in other cases, so in this case he wrote to Mr. Mergenthaler for his opinion upon this subject, at the same time asking him whether he had any recommendations to make for the position. Mr. Mergenthaler replied on the basis outlined above and in a most disinterested way offered to the general manager the services of his own superintendent, under whose direction Mr. Mergenthaler was able to furnish machines to the company at a profit to himself for the sum of $1,050, while the machines produced at the company's own works at that time cost nearly double that sum. There was absolutely no reason why this man could not do the same thing for the company, and any other ordinary business man would have availed himself of so fine an opportunity with pleasure.

Not so, Mr. Dodge; like Mr. Reid in 1888 so he in 1892, went to the outside and engaged a man as superintendent who never before had seen a linotype and who had to get years of experience before he could give as efficient services as the party recommended by Mr. Mergenthaler would have given at once. To complete the parallelism between Mr. Reid's blunder in 1888 and Mr. Dodge's in 1892, the new superintendent in turn engaged as assistant superintendent another outsider likewise entirely unfamiliar with the linotype. It is true that finally both of these gentlemen rendered efficient services, but it took years and many tens of thousands if not hundreds of thousands of dollars before the Brooklyn factory approached the efficiency which already prevailed at Mr. Mergenthaler's works and which by offering his own superintendent he so disinterestedly placed at the company's disposal.

Not satisfied with the first experience, Mr. Dodge a few years later repeated this performance by appointing another outsider to the position of assistant superintendent which had become vacant by the resignation of that official.

Early in 1893 another effort was made to rob the inventor of what little royalty he collected under the modified contract with the Mergenthaler Linotype Company. The Shucker's justifier patents had become more and more threatening and Mr. Mergenthaler's earnest and persistent efforts to invent another practical method of justification had not so far been crowned with success. It was this condition of things which the president of the company now seized upon as an opportunity to further squeeze the inventor and enrich the millionaires in whose interest he had spent seventeen of the best years of his life, and in whose interest he had ruined his health.

Of the many contemptible attempts which to date had been made to take advantage of him none left Mr. Mergenthaler with as much disgust as this one, not perhaps because the others were not equally unjust, but simply because the ground on which it was based was so absurd as to imply an impeachment of either his own sanity or that of the management of the company. Let the letter speak for itself.

NEW YORK, July 13, 1893.

Mr. Ott. Mergenthaler.
    Cor. Claggett and Allen streets,
        Baltimore, Md.

DEAR SIR:

New justification.—There is considerable anxiety among the company officers and others as to whether you can overcome the Shuckers justification, and if so, how soon. They are particularly anxious to know how soon the present machine will be completed as to justifier, and whether you consider that it will be a reliable substitute which can be introduced into our existing machines.

In view of the fact that the justifying devices are an essential and necessary part of the machine, without which it would be inoperative, they of course feel that it was one of the essential things on which the royalty of $50 was based, and that if they have got to put something else in order to make the machine operative at all this fact should be taken into consideration as to payments made you for royalty.

Yours truly,
MERGENTHALER LINOTYPE COMPANY,
PHIL. T. DODGE, <i>Prest. and Gen. Mangr.</i>

"Another one of Mr. Reid's contributions to the castle on the Rhine," Mr. Mergenthaler exclaimed and without much delay informed the company that fortunately his relations with the company were not depending on the "opinions and sentiments of its officers," but were regulated by a written contract, the provisions of which he intended to enforce.

In answer to this Mr. Dodge replied as follows:

Mr. Ott. Mergenthaler.
    Cor. Claggett and Allen streets,
        Baltimore, Md.

DEAR SIR:

Sorts Attachment.—I note that this apparatus has been sent to the Brooklyn factory.

Justification.—I note your remarks on this subject; also the matter of contracts. I also appreciate that the company paid you the large amounts, and contracted to pay the royalty at a time when it was supposed that you were giving them a complete machine which they would have a right to make, and not one which would be an infringement of other patents, or which could not be built without being amenable to other people. I note your remarks that the company has not protected you in your creations with patents. The company has fully protected whatever you have completed and done of value. It has not protected you in things which were invented and patented by others and judicially decided to be the property of others.

For a period of eleven months no royalty was paid and every demand for payment was studiously ignored by the company. Inasmuch as at least one of the directors (Mr. W. C. Whitney) has since denied that the letter in question implied anything of the kind Mr. Mergenthaler inferred from it, we leave it to the reader to give it his own construction and to decide for himself whether the language used and the subsequent suspension of royalty payments, together with the company's failure to acknowledge the receipt of demands, can be construed as anything else than an attempt to saddle the cost of the justification patents upon the inventor. What this really implied the reader will be better able to judge after he is informed that when the Mergenthaler Company finally bought the Shucker's patent it paid therefor the modest little sum of $416,000, an amount more than twice as much as the total royalties collected by the inventor to date and probably more than he or his family will ever be able to collect as the result of his inventions.

In the meantime the monoline machine had made considerable progress; its promoters had several machines built and one of them had been exhibited at the Chicago Exposition. Mr. Mergenthaler himself as early as the fall of 1891 had invented a machine which proved to be practically the same machine as the monoline, and when his application reached the Patent Office an interference was declared between his own and the application of Mr. Scudder. The first hearing in the case took place in the fall of 1893 and at the conclusion of the testimony Mr. Dodge expressed himself to Mr. Mergenthaler as follows: "The only, and the only thing against us in this case is the fact that we did not develop our invention while the other parties did. It has become more and more the practice of the Patent Office to award an invention in controversy to the party which reduces its invention to practice."

A stronger impeachment of his course in this case could not be drawn up by his most severe critics as is implied in the above admission. Here we have the president and general manager with almost unlimited power and means sitting calmly by and seeing intending competitors develop a machine which he knew from the very day he assumed his duties as manager was supposed to be really the invention of Mr. Mergenthaler, and thus enabling the monoline people to get a standing in the Patent Office which they never would have had if he had given authority to develop Mr. Mergenthaler's machine.

The greatest objection to the use of the linotype as developed by actual use was in Mr. Mergenthaler's opinion the burrs which show up in the linotype print after comparatively short use of the matrices, and he never tired of urging upon the company the importance of remedying this worst of all defects by the production of more serviceable matrices. As early as 1890 he made an experimental lot of hardened steel matrices and tried them in a machine with very gratifying results. However, Mr. Dodge failed entirely to appreciate the great improvement which a more serviceable matrix would effect in the appearance of the linotype print, and the great extent to which the innovation advocated would enlarge the field of usefulness in the book printing trade, and finally Mr. Mergenthaler became convinced that under his management the company could not be induced to spend any money towards the production of hardened steel matrices. Here again Mr. Mergenthaler staked his own time and money and started to solve the problem at his own risk.

After working on the problem for some time Mr. Dodge, in December, 1893, called at the Baltimore factory and Mr. Mergenthaler took pleasure as well as pride in showing him how he had progressed on the steel matrix plant which if successful would in his opinion be of immense importance to the company. Not a word of encouragement left the manager's lips, he looked at the machinery and finally said, "Yes, if it can be done it ought to be done."

A few days later a letter was received from him setting out "that on his late visit to Baltimore certain machines were shown him as being constructed for the purpose of making steel matrices, that the matrices were an article covered by patents, that his company had large lots of brass matrices on hand and were also possessed of a very expensive plant for the manufacture of these matrices. In view of these facts, he thought it well to warn Mr. Mergenthaler that his company would permit nothing which would interfere with the company's matrix business or render the stock of matrices and the company's matrix plant less valuable."

Mr. Mergenthaler in answer to this pointed out that the solution of the steel matrix question would be of immense value to the company, that for years he had urged the company to attack the problem themselves, failing in which he had finally concluded to risk the solution of the problem at his own expense. If a failure, the company would not lose anything, and if a success, he had no doubt that the company would either be glad to buy the plant or make arrangements with him to produce hardened steel matrices for the company. Years were spent on the problem and tens of thousands of dollars in the construction of several dozens of special machines, nearly all of them working entirely automatically.

The problem is solved, a hardened steel matrix has been produced at a cost but little above the cost of brass matrices, their wearing qualities have been demonstrated to be far above the brass matrices, but the company to date could not be induced to either buy the plant or to allow Mr. Mergenthaler to bring these matrices into the market on his own account although he offered to pay a royalty of $\frac{1}{4}$ of one cent on each matrix and to run the business without requiring the company to incur any risk in the matter in any way, shape or form.

In January, 1894, a perfectly practical method of justification by step justifiers had been devised by Mr. Mergenthaler which led to the construction of 225 machines of this class which were all made in Baltimore. It was thought at that time with this invention in the possession of the company comparatively easy terms could be made with the owners of the Shucker's patent, or the use of the latter entirely dispensed with, but although the machines in question gave uniform and entire satisfaction, the company now bought the wedge justifier, and paying therefor the enormous sum of $416,000, which is more than any sum ever named before the company had the choice of avoiding the purchase of the Shucker's patent.

In June, 1894, Mr. Mergenthaler brought out the two-line letter for use in small advertisements, which advanced the usefulness of the machine another point and overcame the objection of quite a number of newspaper men. By this time Mr.

Mergenthaler's health had been seriously impaired and his physicians now confessed that he was suffering from pulmonary consumption, thus confirming what he had feared to be the cause of his failing health for several years past. On their advice he spent the balance of the summer in the Blue Mountains, Md., and later in the season removed with his family to Saranac Lake in the Adirondack Mountains, N. Y.

While he was suffering from the first shock induced by realizing the real condition he was in, the National Typographic Company sold the English interests without attempting to make any provision for the royalty to which he was entitled. A demand for a settlement brought the answer that that company did not think that the inventor had a legal claim against them and entirely repudiated all liability. It was found impossible to get the company to define the reasons on which they expected to escape their just debts, and the time not permitting of getting legal advice, and as stated before Mr. Mergenthaler being sick and not in a condition to subject himself to the tribulations of legal proceedings, he accepted as a compromise the sum of $16,000 in full for all his claims under the English patents. Thus again the company took advantage of even the poor state of the inventor's health and escaped its liability by paying about one-tenth of what they were liable for under the contract under which they became possessed of these patents. Another stone toward Mr. Reid's castle on the Rhine!

While he was living in the Adirondacks, the Baltimore factory was carried on under the direction of Mr. Carl Muehleisen as superintendent, and F. Cadell as general foreman. Both of these gentlemen have been with Mr. Mergenthaler for many years, are thoroughly familiar with the Linotype, and men who, like Mr. Mergenthaler himself, are used to paying personal attention to every detail of the business.

It is now nearly four years since Mr. Mergenthaler was compelled to relinquish personal control of the factory, yet with the assistance of the two gentlemen named he managed to continue the business which he loves and which he hopes to preserve for the benefit of his three promising sons who are rapidly approaching the age when they may step in and continue the work of their father, much of which has been cut short, either by the precarious state of his health or by the unfriendly spirit he had to encounter on the part of the company whose duty it would be to develop his inventions.

In July, 1894, an attempt was made to sell the patents of Germany and Austria, which were in litigation on account of failure to introduce the machines in these countries into practical use, the monoline and typograph interest being the attacking parties. It was with a view of saving these patents that Mr. Dodge was sent to Germany with instructions to sell the patents and thereby create an interest in these countries which would start the manufacture of the machines. The price to be paid was to be at least $300,000 in cash. Mr. Dodge was given a power of attorney and he left for Germany. While there he bartered away these patents on conditions entirely at variance with the terms under which he was authorized to sell.

Instead of selling he entered into an agreement by which the patents were transferred to a party by the name of Aug. Scherl on a royalty agreement depending entirely on Scherl's ability to manufacture and sell machines in these countries. Not one cent of money was to be paid by Scherl unless he sold machines, and there was not only no personal obligation on the part of Scherl, but it was specifically stated that Scherl was entering into this agreement on the part of a company *to be organized* by him, and that the agreement should have no binding force against him personally. More than that, this remarkable agreement stipulated that even the company *to be organized* should have the right to abandon the enterprise at any time, but that, on the other hand, the National Typographic Company was to guarantee the title of the patent and prevent the introduction of the Rogers Typograph in the countries named.

In return for all the above enumerated obligations on the part of the National Typographic Company, the Scherl Company *to be organized* was to pay a royalty of $250 on the sale of each machine, $166⅔ to the National Typographic Company, and $83⅓ to Phil. T. Dodge as trustee for others interested in the German patents. These payments to continue until the National Typographic Company had received $616,666⅔ and Mr. Dodge $308,333⅓. No provision of any sort was made for the royalty to which the inventor was entitled, and if the National Typographic Company had to pay it out of their share, there was very little left to divide amongst the stockholders. Most of these German patents have since been declared void on account of failure to introduce the machines, and if the board had ratified the above agreement the company would now probably pay damages instead of collecting royalty. However, the board refused to ratify, but the legal complications arising out of this remarkable transaction by Mr. Dodge were such that after considerable delay practically the same agreement was later ratified, but striking out the little sum of $308,333⅓ for Mr. Dodge and the clause which guaranteed the title to the patent.

A committee of the National Typographic Company has since offered to Mr. Mergenthaler the magnificent sum of $10,000 as a compromise payment in full for royalty which may become due under the German and Austrian patents, and the Mergenthaler Company has recorded itself as not liable for anything in Germany. At the same time the latter company refused to make any further payments on royalties accrued in Canada for the reason that the company had not received any benefits from these patents.

Repudiation over and over again! Mr. Mergenthaler's right to royalty depends on the delivery of machines to the user thereof and not upon the question of the Mergenthaler Company making money out of these patents. If the company made bad bargains, as they did in every foreign country, it is their business and not that of the inventor.

The first dividend was paid in the summer of 1894, the number of machines either sold or on lease at the close of the business year amounting to nearly fifteen hundred and increasing at a very rapid rate, it soon became evident that the dividends would ere long reach quite unusual heights and in order to avoid a possible public outcry of "extortion by a monopoly" it was decided to again resort to the familiar process of watering the stock. The first million of the company's stock consisted of about eight parts water and two parts cash. The second million was all cash. These two millions in 1891 were watered into five millions, only three hundred and seventy-five thousand dollars being put into the treasury in return of the additional stock issued, and this already much diluted mixture was now again subjected to the process of a further watering to the extent of 100 per cent, thus giving each shareholder two shares for each one held before. The company now proposed to pay dividends on a capital of ten million dollars. It was clear to all that ere long the dividends even on this enormously inflated capitalization would get very high, and so they did, having at the time of this writing reached the rate of 20 per cent.

It was now clearly demonstrated that the original royalty to the inventor of ten per cent on the cost of the machine would not only not have crippled the company, but that the earning power of the invention was such that the stockholders would not feel the difference between it and the reduction secured later under the plea that the company could not bear the burden. The company as we have shown never furnished the equivalents which it promised Mr. Mergenthaler in return for this reduction, and it really would not be expecting too much if the reader should conclude that this would be a very good period for the company to show its appreciation of the liberality the inventor had shown it by restoring to him the original royalty.

A surprise was in store for him, but it was not of the kind the reader would be likely to expect. The following correspondence will explain itself:

NEW YORK, October 19, 1895.

Ottmar Mergenthaler, Esq.,
        Baltimore, Md.

DEAR MR. MERGENTHALER:

In considering the new organization it is practically necessary for us to give the new company a new name. It has been found that the present name is so very long as to cause us much inconvenience. We find almost daily that the first part of the name is misspelt in checks, drafts and other papers. Again, the writing of this name, as frequently happens four or five hundred times a day by one person, involves a serious amount of labor. All things considered, it is thought best to call the new company simply the Linotype Company, but of course we do not feel like making any change without consulting you in the matter. There is no desire on our part to detract from the credit which belongs to you, or to lessen the publicity which is given your name. Of course in all our headings and advertising matter, and everywhere else, we shall continue to use your name just as we are already doing. I write you at this time, and before any final action is taken in the matter, so that you may not misunderstand our motives, or may not think that we are in any way trying to reflect on you or to detract from the credit and honor which belongs to you. Yours truly,

P. T. DODGE, G. H. S.

October 23, 1895.

DEAR MR. DODGE:

Of the many communications received from yourself or from the company you represent, I do not remember one which has made so painful an impression upon me as the one contained in your letter of the 19th, advising me of the intention to strike my name from the official title of the proposed new company. The reasons advanced are, putting it mildly, whimsical. To deprive a man who has given to the world one of the most important inventions of the age of the credit therefor by discontinuing his name, seems to me to be an act unworthy of the stockholders, who have been so greatly benefited by my labors, and doubly so if that act comes coincident to the doubling of the capital stock of the company. From an original investment of no more than one and one-half millions, the company has prospered until now it is proposed to pay interest on ten millions, and on the eve of this event, and as a fitting reward for my labors, you propose to strike my name from the title of the company, for no other reasons than that it is sometimes misspelled and that it is rather long.

It would be interesting to know how much the company is likely to be damaged by reason of the misspelling, and how much clerk hire it could dispense with if the name be discontinued.

The company has borne my name during periods when it brought me more ridicule than honor and more aspersions than credit. It has borne it later, and has demonstrated that its name is not inimical to its success. To strike it off now will be a serious and ill-deserved blow and reflection upon me, and the pain caused thereby will be mitigated but little by your assurance that the blow is not intended to hurt me, but that you have to strike me down simply because I am in the way of your catching the fly on the wall.

After all, it seems to be a doubtful policy for a company to materially change its name, under which it has been known and advertised all over the country for the last ten years, and under which it received quite a number of important court decisions.

That the name "Mergenthaler" at the present time is not an obscure and unfamiliar one, but to the contrary, is known to every publisher and printer all over the country, is best shown by the frequent references in trade journals and newspapers in which the machines are referred to quite as frequently as "Mergenthalers" than as Linotypes.

In conclusion I beg to submit for consideration the fact that the exploiters of every other important invention are honoring the inventor by giving his name to their company. Take the Bell Co., the different Edison inventions, the Westinghouse, the McCormick and others, they all carry the inventor's name.

Hoping that I may be spared the intended humiliation, I am, Yours truly,

OTT. MERGENTHALER.

From Mr. Dodge's letter it would appear that he intended to advocate the change only with the consent of the inventor. However, after receiving Mr. Mergenthaler's protest he agitated his plan as energetically as before, thus showing his assurance of good will to have been nothing but hollow pretence. Mr. Mergenthaler at once wrote to Mr. D. O. Mills, whose word was then and is to this day law for the company, protesting against the infamous proposition and appealing to his sense of justice to prevent the scheme from being carried through. Be it said to his honor that in this case for the first time he decided in favor of the inventor and against Mr. Dodge, thus breaking the monotony of his general policy of non-interference and of letting good enough alone.

Probably most of our readers are familiar with the story of the drummer who, as an illustration of the immensity of the business done by his firm, told his customers that the consumption of writing ink was becoming quite a serious expense and that it was now proposed to effect a material reduction of expenses by omitting in future the dot above the i in all of the firm's writings.

This story is a good joke for an ambitious drummer, but here we have the president and general manager of a big company proposing in all seriousness to benefit the company by lessening the clerical labor required in writing the corporate name of the company.

Mr. Dodge's action in this matter resulted in a complete rupture of Mr. Mergenthaler's relations with the president and general manager of the company, which relations, as will be perceived from former pages, had become more and more strained as time had passed and opportunity afforded to Mr. Dodge to exhibit his many shortcomings in the management of Mr. Mergenthaler's patent cases and his enmity to him and his interests as inventor.

There are now in use in the United States, Australia, Germany and other foreign countries over 4000 machines. In England the machines have been manufactured and introduced quite extensively, but no royalty being paid on machines made there, the inventor has no record as to the number of machines in use in that country. Doubtless the number will come close to two thousand.

INDEX.

	PAGE
Biography of Mr. Mergenthaler	3
The evolution of the lithographic rotary machine	4
Biography of Mr. James O. Clephane (the first promoter of the Linotype)	5
The change to the rotary stereotypic system	7
Mr. L. G. Hine's entry into the enterprise	11
First start on the Linotype proper	13
The direct casting machine	15
Substance of Mr. Mergenthaler's contract with the Company	18
Mergenthaler's opinion of the value of his invention, and his hopes and prophecies for its future, as held in 1885	19
The single matrix machine, and advent of the Syndicate	21
The organization of the Mergenthaler Printing Co.	24
First Linotype used on commercial work	26
The matrix problem	29
The baleful work of the Syndicate	33
Mergenthaler's resignation as manager of the Company	36
Difficulties in getting his tools and royalty due him	39
The Syndicate contracts with itself for the free use of Linotype machines	44
The design of the present machine	49
Mr. Hine's management	52
The mistake of Mergenthaler's life	54
Mr. Dodge's management	62
Steel matrices	68
Foreign patents	70
Proposed change in the name of the Company	72

(Editor's Note: In this edition, the pages have been slightly renumbered from the original book because the photos are now included as running pages. In the original they were unnumbered inserts.
On Pages 9, 14, 16, 23 and 57 explanatory words have been added below the patent drawings to aid the reader.)

INTRODUCTORY LETTER PRINTED IN THE CATALOGUE AT RIGHT

BALTIMORE, MARYLAND, 1898.

GENTLEMEN: In presenting this catalogue we desire to announce that we have entered extensively into the manufacture of separate parts for the Linotype machine, an enterprise which we have carried on to a limited extent for several years. Owing to the fact that our dealings in this line have heretofore been transacted through the medium of the Mergenthaler Linotype Co., it is not generally known that we ourselves manufacture and sell directly to users the articles shown in this catalogue, as well as many others.

We, therefore, adopt this means of advertising this fact, and of correcting the general and false impression that all accessories and separate parts of the Linotype must be procured through the same channel through which the machine itself is secured. Repair parts are not protected or monopolized.

The Linotype machine was invented and designed at our works, has been developed and improved by us for years, and we are still engaged upon further improvements. During all this time we have not only manufactured hundreds of them, but have also made a great number of tools designed especially for the accurate and economical production of Linotype parts, and we are, therefore, in a position to furnish the best of this class of work, and guarantee that all supplies, etc., purchased of us will be interchangeable, whether for Baltimore or Brooklyn made machines.

As the Linotype machine (as a whole) will be controlled by a monopoly for several years to come, we do not at present build new machines, but we handle secondhand ones, and make such new parts, etc., as experience has shown to be most liable to breakage and wear, also those attachments, accessories, etc., which are more or less needed in every Linotype office, and which are not covered by the patents of the Mergenthaler Linotype Company.

We have not illustrated each and every part of the machine, but have shown all the essentials, classifying and arranging them in a manner convenient and comprehensive.

We also give views of the various departments of our works, where, in addition to the manufacture of Linotype supplies, we conduct a general machine business, giving particular attention to designing and making automatic machinery of every description, special tools, models, etc.

We solicit the patronage of every office using the Linotype, feeling sure that those who avail themselves of the benefit of our vast experience will be thoroughly satisfied.

Very respectfully,
OTT. MERGENTHALER & CO.,
C. Muehleisen, Manager.

ADDRESS ALL ORDERS DIRECT TO
OTT. MERGENTHALER & CO.
BALTIMORE, MD.

VARIOUS Department Views

OF THE WORKS

OF

OTT. MERGENTHALER & CO.,

THE BIRTHPLACE

OF THE

LINOTYPE MACHINE,

BALTIMORE, MD.

FACTORY (FRONT VIEW).

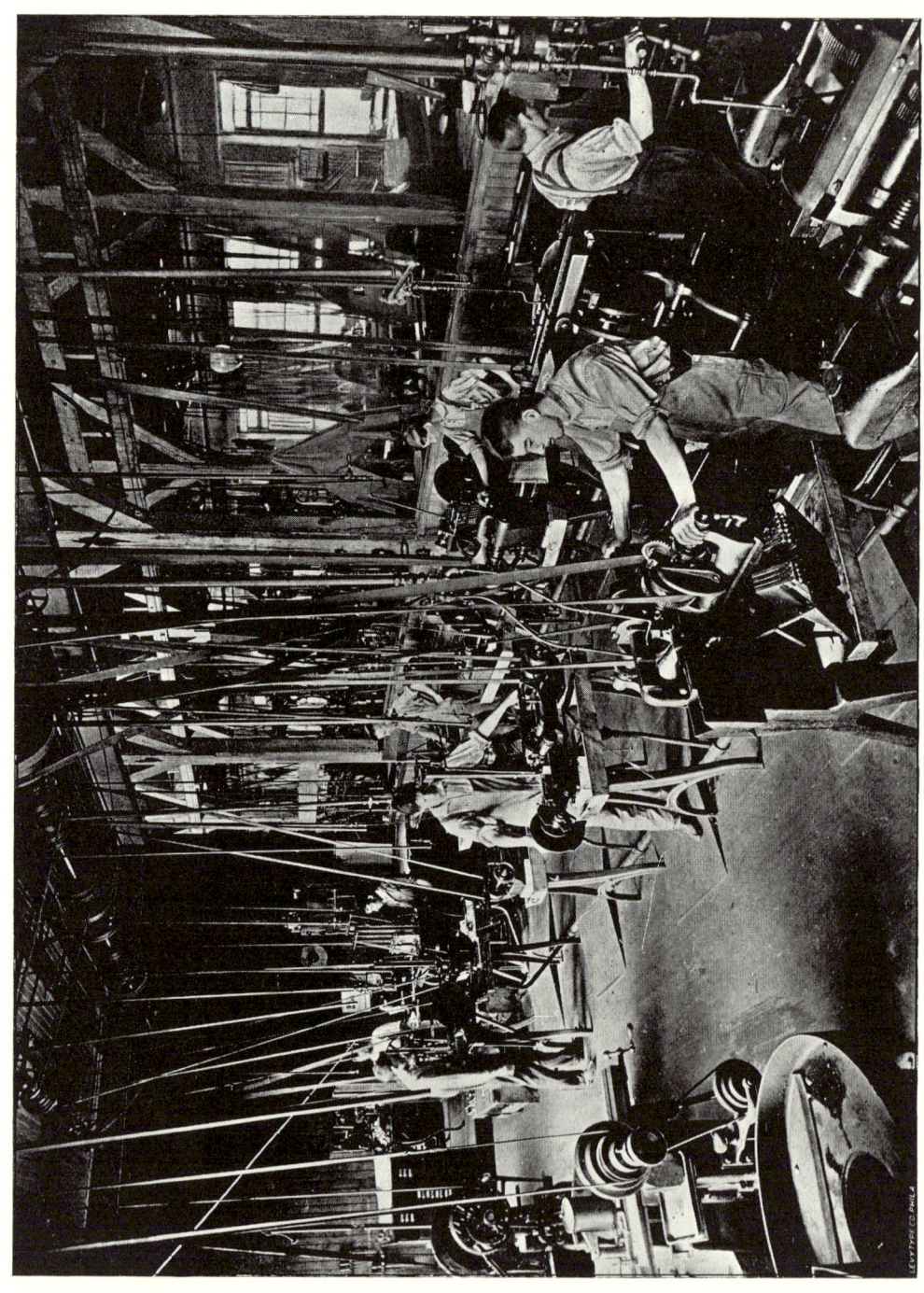

STEEL MATRIX DEPARTMENT.

Steel Matrix Department.

❧ ❧ ❧ ❧ ❧ ❧ ❧

In this department we have been engaged for a number of years in efforts to produce matrices of better wearing qualities than those made of brass, which so far were the only kind used in the Mergenthaler machine.

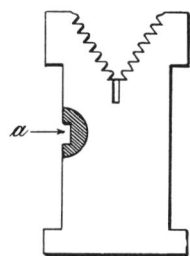

We now have solved the problem by using soft steel and hardening the matrix around the impression point, as indicated in the cut at *a*, which is the most delicate portion of the matrix and contains the fine side walls that encircle the letter.

The brass matrices bend in at this place, resulting in the ill-reputed burrs or hair lines between the letters. The steel matrices largely do away with this nuisance, as they are hardened all around the letter, which greatly increases their strength and durability.

The various special automatic machines and tools of this department have been especially designed and made by us for the accurate and economical production of steel matrices, which renders their manufacture possible at a cost not much in excess of that of brass matrices.

It is a matter of regret that the Mergenthaler Linotype Co. of New York has not yet seen fit to place on the market the steel matrix, which is such a great improvement on the brass one.

EXPERIMENTING ROOM.

Experimenting Room.

In this Room all our

VARIOUS

IMPROVEMENTS

on the Linotype machine are experimented upon and tested, before they are placed on the market.

FURTHER

IMPROVEMENTS

are being made, to meet the needs and requirements of modern printing offices, which are progressing every day.

WE RECOGNIZE THIS FACT

AND LOOK OUT FOR IT.

84

PORTION OF THE OFFICE.

SPECIAL ATTENTION IS CALLED TO OUR

Designing and Drafting Department,

IN WHICH, IN ADDITION TO THE LINOTYPE WORK,

We Design to Order

All Kinds of Automatic Machinery,

Special Tools, Models, etc.

The fact that WE DESIGNED THE LINOTYPE, one of the most ingenious machines, seems to offer REASONABLE GUARAN= TEE that the interests of our patrons will be well served by entrusting to us the DESIGNING OF ANY NEW MACHINERY for which they may feel a want in their particular line of business.

In his own handwriting, shown at right, inventor Ottmar Mergenthaler describes the images below, proofed from printing bars, as being "Made July 15, 1885. on first machine with independent matrices." A patent drawing of this machine is on page 23. The term "printing bar" was used before "Linotype slug" came into being in 1886.
—proof sheet courtesy of Linotype Company archives

Ott. Mergenthaler Greetings to L. G. Hine Esq.
Ott. Mergenthaler Greetings to L. G. Hine Esq.
Ott. Mergenthaler Greetings to L. G. Hine Esq.
Ott. Mergenthaler Greetings to L. G. Hine Esq.
Ott. Mergenthaler Greetings to L. G. Hine Esq.
Ott. Mergenthaler Greetings to L. G. Hine Esq.
Ott. Mergenthaler Greetings to L. G. Hine Esq.
Ott. Mergenthaler Greetings to L. G. Hine Esq.
Ott. Mergenthaler Greetings to L. G. Hine Esq.
Ott. Mergenthaler Greetings to L. G. Hine Esq.
Ott. Mergenthaler Greetings to L. G. Hine Esq.
Ott. Mergenthaler Greetings to L. G. Hine Esq.
Ott. Mergenthaler Greetings to L. G. Hine Esq.
Ott. Mergenthaler Greetings to L. G. Hine Esq.
Ott. Mergenthaler Greetings to L. G. Hine Esq.
Ott. Mergenthaler Greetings to L. G. Hine Esq.
Ott. Mergenthaler Greetings to L. G. Hine Esq.
Ott. Mergenthaler Greetings to L. G. Hine Esq.
Ott. Mergenthaler Greetings to L. G. Hine Esq.
Ott. Mergenthaler Greetings to L. G. Hine Esq.
Ott. Mergenthaler Greetings to L. G. Hine Esq.
Ott. Mergenthaler Greetings to L. G. Hine Esq.
Ott. Mergenthaler Greetings to L. G. Hine Esq.
Ott. Mergenthaler Greetings to L. G. Hine Esq.
Ott. Mergenthaler Greetings to L. G. Hine Esq.
Ott. Mergenthaler Greetings to L. G. Hine Esq.
Ott. Mergenthaler Greetings to L. G. Hine Esq.
Ott. Mergenthaler Greetings to L. G. Hine Esq.
Ott. Mergenthaler Greetings to L. G. Hine Esq.
Ott. Mergenthaler Greetings to L. G. Hine Esq.
Ott. Mergenthaler Greetings to L. G. Hine Esq.
Ott. Mergenthaler Greetings to L. G. Hine Esq.
Ott. Mergenthaler Greetings to L. G. Hine Esq.
Ott. Mergenthaler Greetings to L. G. Hine Esq.
Ott. Mergenthaler Greetings to L. G. Hine Esq.
Ott. Mergenthaler Greetings to L. G. Hine Esq.
Ott. Mergenthaler Greetings to L. G. Hine Esq.
Ott. Mergenthaler Greetings to L. G. Hine Esq.
Ott. Mergenthaler Greetings to L. G. Hine Esq.
Ott. Mergenthaler Greetings to L. G. Hine Esq.

PART II
Reprint of the first major story about the Linotype ever published:

New-York Tribune. SUNDAY EDITION. MAY 19, 1889.

THE LINOTYPE.

A REVOLUTION IN PRINTING.

THE LATEST TRIUMPH OF AMERICAN INVENTION SEEN IN THE TRIBUNE OFFICE.

MOVABLE TYPES DISPENSED WITH—
A MACHINE ALMOST HUMAN IN ITS ACTION—
A STORY OF PATIENT ENDEAVOR AND COMPLETE SUCCESS.

When people talk about the marvels of printing and the changes wrought by recent improvements in the art, they generally forget that one branch of it has remained hitherto undeveloped. The discovery of stereotyping and the perfection of the cylinder press, which cuts, folds and pastes and throws off the printed sheets faster than one can count, have revolutionized the industry within the memory of man. Yet the problem of typesetting by machinery has resisted nearly every effort at solution, and the present hand-compositor on a New-York daily employs precisely the same methods to "set up" a special Centennial edition that Gutenberg used in his early essays at Strasburg four centuries ago.

The New-York Tribune, the first American newspaper to stereotype and the first to print from a Hoe perfecting press, is the first to announce a successful departure from this old and tedious system. For nearly three years it has been introducing into its office a machine which dispenses altogether with movable type, and whose adaptability to practical newspaper work, in spite of many discouragements at the outset, is at last satisfactorily demonstrated. The machine now does substantially all the composition of this paper. The old-fashioned frames and trays, with their square compartments filled with dingy types, have given place in its composing-room to upright structures of brass and iron, overhung by a network of belts, long lines of shafting, huge metal pipes and revolving wheels. A new industry has, in fact, arisen, and among The Tribune typesetters the case and stick are already things of the past.

The Tribune's experiments with devices for saving time and labor at the case date back for many years. As long ago as 1866, Mr. Greeley, always hospitable to new ideas, made trials of the Alden machine. This, like the inventions of Mitchel, Delcambre, Fraser and others, was designed merely to duplicate by machinery the motions of the compositor's hands, and, like them, it broke down under the severe test of morning newspaper work. The best of this class of machines were, perhaps, those of the late G. A. Burr, which, up to a few months ago, had been in use in this office for several years. The first was put in in May, 1880, during the lifetime of the inventor and under his supervision, and the number was subsequently increased to three. The results were fairly satisfactory, but there were fatal obstacles to success. In the first place, the original cost was great and the expense of repairs considerable. A specially prepared type was required, which broke easily and wore out very fast. One operator was needed to set the matter, another to justify it, and a third to attend to the distributor (which was a separate piece of machinery). Frequent stoppages were necessary for replenishing the font, and the output of each machine, under the most favorable conditions, was only from 4,000 to 5,000 ems per hour, so that the actual saving was small. Moreover, there were numerous sources of delay, the type "pied" easily, and typographical blunders were unpleasantly common.

ORIGIN OF THE LINOTYPE.

In the fall of 1884, however, a new and wonderful instrument began to be talked about which would found and compose its own type. This instrument was the Linotype, invented at Baltimore, Maryland, by Ottmar Mergenthaler, a native of Wurtemberg, Germany, who was born in 1854, learned the trade of a watchmaker, and came to this country in 1872. Its conception was due primarily to Mr. James O. Clephane, a Washington stenographer, who has made writing and printing machines a hobby for over twenty years, and who, in 1876, employed the engineering firm of which Mr. Mergenthaler was a member to work from drawings by a Western inventor. Mr. Mergenthaler immediately discovered a singular aptitude for this kind of work, and began experimenting with various methods of casting type-bars from matrices made by indentations in soft material, and soon improved upon the crude device originally submitted to him. His first idea took the form of a rotary machine, with keys for impressing female dies in a continuous strip of heavy paper, which was then cut into short lengths for adjustment as the matrix of an entire column or page. This was superseded by a machine controlling a series of sliding bars, each bearing on one edge all the characters and spaces. A key mechanism moved these bars endwise so as to bring a selected character on any bar into line with a selected character on any other, and thus form the matrix of a complete line for casting. It was not until 1880 that a complete change of system was made, and not until 1884 that the machine was finally completed which, in its perfected form, marks such a signal advance over all its predecessors.

In appearance the Linotype has been, not inaptly, likened to an upright piano. It is about five feet long, five feet high, and three feet broad. As is shown by the accompanying cut,* the most conspicuous objects supported by the heavy iron base are a typewriter keyboard and a series of vertical flattened tubes, Each of these tubes or magazines contains a number of short strips of brass, having the mould for a particular character stamped in the further edge. The bottom strip or "matrix" in each tube rests in a slot at the end of the corresponding key; and when this key is depressed, the matrix at once drops in an upright position into a groove or channel, sloping above the keyboard from right to left. A powerful air-blast instantly forces the matrix along a wire which maintains it in its upright position to the lower end of the groove, and here two metallic fingers, working automatically, push it out into full view upon a horizontal slide; and as it is marked on the outer edge with the letter it represents, the operator can correct his work as he goes along. When all the matrices of a word are assembled on the slide, a touch on a particular key brings down a long, thin, wedge-shaped strip, or "space-band." The thicker end of this wedge hangs below the matrices, just over a metal plate, so that when the line is finished the automatic raising of this plate will push the space-bands upward

---

* *A picture of this machine is on page 96.—ED.*

through the line until the different words are all equally divided, and thus the nice process of "justification" is accomplished at a single stroke.

CASTING AND DISTRIBUTING.

The first step is now finished. the line is ready to be cast. But the operator simply moves a lever and goes on with his work at the keys, leaving the machine to do the rest. And it does it quickly and well. As the lever moves, the space-bands spread the words, a pair of clamps seize the line of matrices, remove them from the slide and press them against the face of a vertical disk. Extending horizontally through this disk is a narrow opening, or slot, of the exact length of the required type-bar. Behind it, a small gas furnace keeps a pot-full of type metal constantly at liquid heat; and while the moulded edges of the matrices are held against the disk, an automatic force-pump throws out a jet of molten metal through the slot. In an instant a block is formed, of the size and shape of an ordinary line of types, bearing on its face in relief the letters corresponding to the line of matrices. The disk then makes half a turn; the bar meets a pair of automatic knives which trim it square, and the next moment it is pushed out, solid, but still warm, at the bottom of a galley standing on end against the machine at the operator's left.

But now a series of even more ingenious operations is performed. Each of the matrices which have just been used must be restored to the tube from which it originally came, and in effecting this the machine displays an almost more than human intelligence. An operator entrusted to perform such a task by hand would first pick out the different sorts, then carefully compare them with the tubes, and finally use dexterity in placing them where they belonged. Not so the machine. As soon as a line is cast, it simply withdraws the matrices from their position against the disk and lifts them by automatic carriers to the top of the machine. Here they encounter a sort of endless railroad, or belt, fitted with hanging loops, which catch them up and travel with them from left to right above the tops of the tubes.

The tops of the matrices are cut in the shape of a V, the inner edges of this V being notched in such a manner that all the matrices of the same character are alike, and different from those of any other. As the belt moves along, these Vs closely hug a stationary bar placed between the loops, and fitted with an arrangement of fine ridges, which differs over every tube. These ridges correspond with the notches in the different Vs, in such a way that when a matrix is brought exactly above the tube to which it belongs, it no longer engages any ridges on the bar, the loop ceases to sustain it, and it falls at once into place, ready to be used again. To guard against possible mishaps, the distributing bar is connected with wires from a battery, by means of which the premature dropping of a matrix closes an electric circuit and stops the carrier belt.

The capacity of the machine in the hands of a competent operator is from 3,000 to 5,000 ems per hour, and six weeks are generally sufficient for a person of average intelligence to learn to attain this speed. Its other merits are obvious. It cannot "pi," does not destroy or scatter type, involves no waste, and furnishes a constant supply of new characters. No foreman with experience of the two systems would hesitate for a moment to declare in its favor. The proofs are cleaner and corrections more quickly made, and the product is more easily handled for the make-up. Late copy, brought in half an hour before the paper goes to press, can be given out in much longer "takes," and the operator, having a continuous story before him instead of a mere fragment, loses less time over doubtful words. The difficulty of "beginning and ending even," is moreover greatly diminished, while "pigeonholes"—the wide blanks caused by hurried spacing—cannot possibly occur. The men themselves soon learn to prefer a style of employment which keeps them comfortably seated before a keyboard instead of requiring them to stand all night at the case. The copy is brought much nearer the eye—a genuine boon to a short-sighted "typo," the hands make fewer motions, the arm is never cramped from holding a composing-stick in one position for hours at a time, and the tedious and unprofitable labor of distribution is entirely done away with, and if any conservative old fogy wants proof of the greater neatness of the work under the new conditions, a glance at The Tribune's clear, clean columns and their accurate alignment and almost perfect spacing will supply it.

WORKING FOR PERFECTION.

This perfection has not, however, been attained without great labor and expense. The story of The Tribune's experience is that of all pioneers in an untried field. The first machine was put up in its office in July, 1886. In the January following five had been received, but only two remained in use. The first suffered so many breakages and was of such inferior make that it had to be taken down and rebuilt, while two others were rejected on account of defective parts. Actual operation discovered a multitude of defects which had never before been dreamed of, and, although no radical changes were made, it was found necessary to modify several details of the construction. Indeed, but for The Tribune's faith in the ultimate success of the machine, the experience of the first twelve months would have insured its abandonment; for, to say nothing of breakages and failures, repeated changes in the inventor's plans and delays in supplying machines, the difficulty of training compositors to a duty which they naturally regarded with aversion, was alone discouragement enough. In the instrument itself each day revealed new flaws. For a long time no suitable metal could be procured for casting, nor its temperature satisfactorily controlled. The matrix moulds were untrue; the matrices themselves were warped and constantly blew out of the channel; the metal squirted between them and spoiled the cast; the air-blast was unmanageable; the tubes became clogged, and the operators were poisoned by fumes from the casting-pots; and, when the linotypes were finally produced, they refused to stand upright in the form. The effect on the appearance of the print may be imagined. Long blank spaces disfigured nearly every proof. Dirty streaks made the larger characters illegible and obliterated the small ones altogether. Every line was full of blurs. In some places only one edge had taken the ink. In others the bars were upside down, and occasionally at the most interesting part of an article a line would vanish altogether. Extraordinary pains were necessary to keep mistakes out of the paper, and even then angry letters came in from many indignant readers. Its oldest friends protested against the strain on their eyes and nerves, and the men left at the cases ridiculed the whole contrivance and predicted its speedy consignment to the scrap-heap.

By the beginning of 1888 fourteen machines had been received. Industry had removed some difficulties and experience lessened others; yet serious obstacles were still to be overcome. There was no ready mode of changing the measure. The headings had to be set by hand and the use of italics abandoned altogether, and the simultaneous use of two styles of type made good results impossible. The movable types, elongated by the heat of repeated stereotyping, still took the impression off the shorter type-bars, which, being new every day, retained their proper size; and "The Louisville Courier-Journal" and "Chicago Daily News," which had begun to use the machines, threatened to throw them out on this account alone; while the pressmen to whom The Tribune "Book of Open-Air Sports" was given for printing from linotypes declared that they never had had such a job. But perhaps the most troublesome experience of all was with the matrices. The moulds for these were at first electrotyped from ordinary type, but, after repeated casting, the electrotyped deposit pulled off and left them useless. A machine was then devised to cast them, but no sooner was this completed than it was found that there was no metal at once soft enough to take a good mould and hard enough to be cast from again without melting. Punching with steel dies directly into the face of the brass was the next method tried, but this spread the mould so as to interfere with the justification and prevent impressions of uniform depth; and it was only by the use of a specially hardened brass that satisfactory matrices were at last obtained. As to the metal, an alloy of bismuth, antimony and lead was, after much experimenting, shown to give the best results, and the pots were fitted with covers and chimneys to carry away the fumes.

WHAT MACHINES ARE DOING.

But no improvements wrought much change in the appearance of the paper until it succeeded in training a competent force of operators, and was provided with its present outfit of forty-two machines. Since then it has been all that could be desired. Editorials, news dispatches, city articles, market reports, literary matter and those "little advertisements of the people" which occupy a constantly increasing space in these pages, are all composed by the linotype machines: and only the stock and bond tables, the little court calendar, the heavy display type in the advertisements and the large pica headlines give employment to the four men still at the case. For the small capitals a machine is already built, and a clever operator turns out tabulated matter where no rules are involved about three times as quickly as by manual composition. With only twenty-eight to thirty-four machines—the number found equal to the demands of any night, excepting that of the large Sunday paper—the operators these employ, the machinist who keeps them in order, the foreman and those at the case and make-up, The Tribune accomplishes what under other conditions would require the services of over 100 men; and nothing stronger can be said in favor of the machine than this.

The first cost of so elaborate a plant was, of course, considerable, as were the expenses incident to its installation, and these must be taken into account in any calculation of the economy of the change. A small vertical engine of nominally twelve horse-power, which The Tribune already had in its composing-room, was found inadequate to the demands of the office after twenty-two machines had been put up, the horse-power required for working the distributor, force-pump and other automatic parts being about .17 for each machine. Connection was therefore established by a cable over 300 feet long with the great Corliss engine in the basement, which runs nearly all the machinery in the building, including presses, wetting machines and the machinery of the stereotyping-room, as well as the presses of "The Morning Journal" and the machinery of the Homer Lee Bank Note Company; and about 200 feet of shafting were put up in the composing-room, with a wheel and belt for every machine. A large No. 5 Roots blower was furnished to supply the air-blast for forcing the matrices into the channels. This blower makes 160 revolutions a minute, discharging twenty-three cubic feet of air at every revolution, or 3,680 cubic feet per minute—this amount being greatly increased by a pressure of one pound per square inch above the atmosphere—and is connected with the machines by a heavy galvanized-iron pipe 150 feet long where it enters the composing-room and fifteen inches in diameter throughout its entire length. A complicated system of gas fixtures was also added to each machine, with stop-cocks to connect them with the draft and regulate the force-blast for the furnace. The chimneys of the casting-pots were connected with a large main flue leading to the roof, and incandescent electric lights were brought before each machine. Besides the cost of these fixtures must be reckoned the current outlay for gas consumed, amounting in the case of The Tribune to 270,000 feet per month; the expense of new type-metal; new matrices; cost of training operators; royalties on machines; wages of machinists for repairing damage caused by the hard usage the machines receive from beginners, and interest on the capital invested. It should, however, be said that the sum paid for the lease of the machines and for fitting them in position for actual work in an office where steam is already used, is much below the first cost of the type, cases, and other paraphernalia required to equip an ordinary composing-room to do an equal amount of work; while the running expenses enumerated above are nearly if not quite set off by the saving in the wear and breakage of the type in ordinary work at the case.

FIGURES OF EXPENSE AND PROFIT.

The most accurate idea of the real working of the machines is to be gleaned from the actual figures, and these are also interesting as showing the costliness of The Tribune's experiment. In 1884 and 1885, when they were not in use, the composing-room expenses were $73,176.26 and $75,070.16 respectively. In 1886, the year of their introduction, these had risen to $86,009.71, and in 1887 they were still $83,475.37, or in the neighborhood of $10,000 above the average of former years. A report for the first week in February, 1888, when eighteen operators were at work, showed an average composition of 101,000 ems per man, at an average cost of 21 cents—the highest amount paid by any operator being $46.45, and the lowest $9, to a beginner whose proportion was small. For the week ending March 28, 1888, 29 operators set an average of 86,200 ems, costing an average of 26 cents per thousand. During this week the two most expert operators composed a number of intricate tables, somewhat reducing the total cost of their work.

During the first week of May, 31 operators set 2,777,000 ems, which cost $656.90. One operator made the especially low rate of 13 cents per thousand, two of 16 cents, one of 17 cents and five of 19 cents. In other words, one-third of the total force averaged below 20 cents; yet the whole average was not less than 23 2/3 cents. Thirty-eight operators set, during the second week in October, an average of 104,000 ems each, at an average cost of 20.2 cents, at which figure, or a little over, it remained until the week ending November 14, when 34 men set an average of 102,000 ems, the cost of which was 19.5 cents per thousand. The lowest average during 1888 was that for the week ending December 12, when 35 operators set an average of 108,400, the average cost per thousand being 18.7 cents.

Since the beginning of 1889, the ordinary weekly record has varied from an average of 116,400 ems set by 31 operators and costing an average of 17.8 cents to 110,000 ems set by 32 operators and costing 19.8 cents. The following table of corrected ems set up by the entire force of 34 operators for a period of four consecutive weeks in March, shows averages for different men ranging from 9½ cents to 24 4/10 cents per thousand:

Operators.	Number of Ems set.	Av'ge per W'k.	Earned per W'k	Cost per 1,000 Ems.
Adams	412,500	103.1	$18.00	17.4 cts.
Allen	431,500	107.8	20.00	18.5
Babcock	493,000	123.2	12.00	9.5
Balls	600,00	150.0	25.00	16.6
Barron*	77,500	77.5	21.00	27.0
Beekman	533,200	133.3	26.00	19.5
Bevan	387,000	96.7	18.00	18.6

Operators.	Number of Ems set.	Av'ge per W'k.	Earned per W'k	Cost per 1,000 Ems.
Brady	286,000	71.5	13.00	18.1 cts.
Brandenburg	423,000	107.0	25.00	23.00
Bussey	410,700	102.6	21.00	20.4
Collins	502,600	125.6	26.00	20.7
Dunlap	483,600	120.9	25.50	21.0
Good	419,800	104.9	12.00	11.4
Hammel	510,000	127.5	25.00	19.6
Henry**	154,800	77.4	12.00	15.5
Hudnut**	144,100	72.0	15.00	20.8
Jarvis	520,500	130.1	16.65	16.1
Jolley	321,000	107.0	23.50	21.9
Ketcham	435,500	108.8	18.00	16.5
Keller***	335,000	111.6	26.00	23.2
McCormack	516,100	129.0	26.00	20.1
McFeeley*	348,400	116.1	13.15	11.3
Miller, J.	549,400	137.3	26.00	19.0
Miller, T.	460,000	115.0	26.00	22.6
Mills	529,000	132.2	25.00	18.9
Rudolph**	225,000	112.5	27.50	24.4
Shike	455,000	113.7	22.50	19.8
Stack***	365,400	121.8	25.50	20.9
Tyler	430,000	107.5	25.00	22.9
Tuthill***	385,000	128.3	25.00	19.6
Vincent	348,700	87.1	10.80	12.4
Wardell	434,600	108.6	25.00	23.0
Wells	415,700	103.9	18.00	17.3
Wooley	534,500	133.6	26.00	19.4

——— *One week.
**Two weeks.
***Three weeks.

The report for the week ending April 3 showed the following results:

Operator.	Amount set.	Amount paid.	Cost per 1,000.
Adams	134.0	$21.00	15.6
Babcock	104.0	13.00	12.5
Balls	148.0	25.00	16.8
Beekman	111.6	26.00	23.2
Bevan	95.0	18.00	18.9
Brady	74.0	13.00	17.6
Brandenburg	120.0	26.25	21.8
Bussey	109.0	20.00	18.3
Collins	119.0	25.75	21.7
Cottingham	130.1	16.80	12.9
Dunlap	119.5	25.00	20.9
Good	110.2	12.00	10.8
Hammel	140.0	25.75	18.3
Henry	76.5	12.00	15.6
Hudnut	76.4	15.00	19.6
Jarvis	126.0	21.00	16.6
Jolley	126.0	23.00	19.0
Keller	123.0	26.00	21.1
Ketcham	113.3	18.00	15.9
McCormack	132.0	26.00	19.6
McFeeley	106.0	25.75	24.2
Miller, J.	142.0	26.00	18.3
Miller, T.	142.0	25.00	17.6
Mills	115.0	25.00	21.7
Shike	120.0	23.50	19.5
Stack	122.6	26.00	21.2
Tyler	120.0	25.00	20.8
Vincent	84.0	10.80	12.8
Wells	106.0	15.00	14.1
Woolley	104.0	21.85	21.0
Average	114.7		18.5

Owing to the usual and unavoidable delays in the preparation and distribution of copy, the figures given above, while accurately showing the output of the machine in everyday use by a morning newspaper, did not so accurately represent its actual capacity under favorable conditions, Copy for a special trial was, therefore, prepared in advance and continuously supplied to the operators during the week ending April 10, so that for every one of the eight hours of each of six working days, every man was steadily employed. The result, in spite of short waits caused by stoppages of the machinery (which had not been specially adjusted for the trial) was sufficiently startling. It showed that thirty-three operators in forty-eight hours had produced the large aggregate of 4,557,300 ems of corrected matter, or an average of 138,100 ems each; in other words, that the work of one man in 1,584 hours on the machine equalled the work of one man during 3,039 16/30 hours at the case, and this at a cost for actual composition of only 15.4 cents. Including the time necessary for distribution, the total number of hours occupied by the hand workers would amount to something like 4,052; so that the machine increased every man's capacity more than two-and-a-half times, and reduced the cost of his labor to less than one-third of the usual sum. It should be borne in mind that this result was attained without any extra exertion on the part of the operators, or any effort for a spurt of speed. The details are shown in the following table:

Operator.	Amount set.	Amount paid.	Cost per 1,000.
Adams	136.0	$18.00	13.2
Babcock	108.0	10.85	10.0
Balls	192.0	25.00	13.0
Beekman	163.6	25.06	15.2
Bevan	121.3	18.00	14.8
Brady	105.0	13.00	12.3
Brandenburg	158.0	26.00	16.4
Bussey	124.5	22.50	18.0
Collins	155.0	26.00	16.7
Cottingham	126.1	15.80	11.8
Dunlap	151.0	26.00	17.2
Good	129.8	12.00	9.2
Hammel	160.0	26.00	16.2
Henry	98.0	12.00	12.2
Hudnut	98.6	15.00	15.2
Jarvis	157.0	25.35	16.1
Jolley	119.6	23.50	19.6
Keller	150.0	26.00	17.3
Ketcham	135.3	18.00	13.3
McCormack	155.0	26.00	16.7
McFeeley	134.0	26.00	19.4
Miller, J.	169.0	26.00	15.3
Miller, T.	134.0	25.50	19.0
Mills	169.0	25.00	14.7
Shike	149.0	23.50	15.7
Stack	134.6	25.75	19.1
Tyler	152.0	26.00	17.1
Van Leer	133.0	23.25	17.4
Vincent	116.0	10.80	9.3
Wardell	140.9	25.00	17.7
Wells	120.0	15.00	12.5
Wooley	152.0	26.00	17.1
Average	138.1		12.2

The Mergenthaler Printing Company, which was organized for the manufacture and introduction of these machines, has its office in Room 76 of The Tribune Building. L.G. Hine, a well-known Washington lawyer of long business and technical experience, is its president, and personally supervises the details of the construction. Mr. Mergenthaler, the inventor, is also retained by the company as consulting engineer. Its factory, in Ryerson Street, Brooklyn, is admirably equipped for the rapid production of machines, and about 130 have been turned out up to date and supplied to newspapers in Louisville, Chicago, Washington, Philadelphia and Providence, R.I. Connected with the factory is a job office, where operators are trained and sent out from time to time to instruct beginners in offices ordering an outfit. Several novels and other publications have been set up in this job office to the entire satisfaction of all concerned. In book work the advantages of the machine are indeed specially marked, since it produces with ordinary effort the superior quality of work which involves extra care and, therefore, extra expense when done by hand. But its most striking achievements so far have been in the exacting field of the daily newspaper. It has added to the wonderful mechanical resources which make possible the production every few hours of huge broadsides and big editions. It promises to do for the composing-room what Frederick Koenig's steam-press and Robert Hoe's cylinders have done for the press-room; and an enterprising editor can as well afford to neglect it as to neglect those valuable devices for the successful duplication of the printed sheet.

On May 19, 1889, after almost a three-year silence, the New York Tribune published this first story about the newspaper's use of the Linotype in its composing room. The delay seems due to Publisher Whitelaw Reid's reluctance to praise the inventor or his machine publicly. In Mergenthaler's "Biography," the inventor claims (page 53 of this book) that it was pressure from the Linotype Company's new 1889 board of directors that forced publication of this mostly favorable story. It was done to help revitalize the Linotype Company's business, for new orders had fallen to practically none under the chairmanship of Whitelaw Reid.—ED.

The Tribune Building, Home of the First Linotype

In this early 1880's photo, The New York Tribune's two-tone building is the dominating landmark in the city's Printing House Square. At right, in the distance, can be seen the towers of the new Brooklyn Bridge.

The Tribune building faced City Hall. Completed in 1875, it was the city's first office skyscraper. At 260 feet the 100,000-circulation newspaper towered over its rivals The Sun (adjoining the Tribune, left) and The New York Times (right). The area was also called "Newspaper Row."

In 1886 inventor Ottmar Mergenthaler installed his first "Blower" typesetting machine in the Tribune's ninth-floor composing room. The first live stories cast on that equipment were used in the paper's July 3d edition. Because Mergenthaler's typeface was identical to that used by the paper's hand compositors, the historic event escaped detection by readers. The Tribune itself did not mention the transition for almost three years. By then the paper owned forty-two of the successful, newly named "Linotype" machines and composed most of its text on them.

In front of the Tribune, on what is now Pace University Plaza and Park Row, stands a statue of Benjamin Franklin, so-called "patron saint" of American printers. On the yearly anniversary of his birth (Jan. 17, 1706), New York employing printers, union typographers and printing students still hold an observance there in his honor.

The World's First Linotype Operator

John T. Miller, the first person after the inventor to operate the Mergenthaler Linotype, demonstrated his keyboard skills during the company's 50th anniversary celebration in 1936. He recalled his first use of the machine at the New York Tribune half a century before. At the time of the photograph Mr. Miller was a proofreader, working at the New York Herald Tribune.

Miller is seated at one of the earliest "Blower" models, so-called because blasts of air were needed to push the type matrices into the assembler.

Born in Lawrence, Mass., in 1865, Miller was employed as a hand compositor at the Tribune in 1883. Shortly afterwards he learned to operate the Burr composing machine, a two-man device that composed and justified specially-made pieces of hand type. In 1886 Miller was selected to be the first operator on the Mergenthaler slug caster, soon renamed the Linotype.

Miller set the first stories to appear in the newspaper, and also composed the type for the first Linotype-set book, *The Tribune Book of Open-Air Sports,* which was published at the end of 1886.

In the span of a century more than 100,000 Linotypes have been manufactured. If each machine averaged four persons operating it during its useful life of fifty or more years, then a veritable army of Linotypists have followed John Miller in this typesetting skill, created by Mergenthaler's ingenious invention.

Ottmar Mergenthaler, The Inventor As Seen by Three Artists

THE following pages show three artists depicting the same historical event in Ottmar Mergenthaler's life. The author's personal observations are offered in examining these different portrayals.

The first picture (page 98) is of a mural, 8½ feet wide by 16 feet tall. Part of a set of four, it graces the vestibule that leads to the third-floor Catalog Room of the New York Public Library.

Edward Laning (1906-1981) created this "Story of the Recorded Word." His conception fits perfectly with the Library's rich architecture. Laning's style is "academic naturalism," popular in Paris in the 19th century.[1]

The first panel in the set (not shown) pictures Moses carrying the Ten Commandments: "the writing of God, graven on tablets."[2] The second panel shows a monk laboriously copying a manuscript—the handwritten word. Laning's third panel has Gutenberg displaying the first printed word, a Bible page, to Adolph of Nassau.[3] To close his theme Laning used Mergenthaler and his Linotype: words set by machine.

On careful inspection, the artist's work is revealing. The painting's accurate setting shows the new Brooklyn Bridge, some 1880's tenements and a newsboy. In the left foreground, in shadow, sits publisher Whitelaw Reid, inspecting his newspaper, an enthused worker at his side. At lower center lie more pages of the paper, with the top sheet showing the *New York Tribune* masthead and dateline of July 3, 1886—the day of first commercial use of the Linotype to set part of the newspaper.

In the center Mergenthaler is bathed in light, his right arm sprawled over the keyboard of his machine. Lost in thought, perhaps he foresees the great impact his invention would have on civilization. Or maybe he is thinking of the machine as a new servant to man. The inventor once said to his wife about the Linotype, "It's all but human; it only lacks the human mind."[4]

In the lower right corner a scribbled piece of paper lies on the floor. The writing is significant, for it is the artist's farewell message that says "To I.N. Phelps Stokes—Except for his unfailing helpfulness and encouragement/These paintings would not have been./Edward Laning, New York, March 1940."[5]

Page 99 shows a pen and ink drawing by artist J. Coggeshall Wilson. The author first saw this in Sean Jennett's book, *Pioneers in Printing*.[6] Biographical information about the artist is sketchy.[7] We only know he was born in New York City and exhibited in a Paris salon in 1902, taking an honorable mention prize in 1904. Even the book's author could not be located for further clues. Reader information would be welcomed.

The "attitudes" of the two subjects—influential newspaper publisher Whitelaw Reid and small businessman-workman-inventor Ottmar Mergentha-

ler—are interesting. Reid almost dominates the work, by his standing position, his businessman's clothing and his patrician's stance, as he looks down coolly at a seated Mergenthaler. The inventor, in rolled-up sleeves, seems sincerely interested in explaining his machine to his chief financial backer.

Perhaps the artist knew Reid's reputation for natty dressing, his marriage into great wealth and his friendships with the wealthy elite of America. This Linotype event took place in 1886[8]; Reid was appointed Ambassador to France in 1889, ran for Vice President in 1892 and in 1905 became Ambassador to Great Britain. Mergenthaler remained linked to the workingman's world, a skilled mechanical engineer whose invention brought him into contact with "old money" people who did not take them into their circle.

The wood engraving on page 100 was commissioned by the Mergenthaler

Linotype Company in 1961, as part of the 75th anniversary events that marked the typesetter's first use.

The artist, John DePol, one of America's acclaimed contemporary wood engravers, is an illustrator, printmaker and teacher. A self-taught artist, DePol's work is in the collections of the Metropolitan Museum of Art, the Library of Congress, and in many fine books.[9]

DePol said he prepared for his assignment (Whitelaw Reid holding the first printing bar and supposedly exclaiming "Ottmar, you've done it! You've set a line of type!") by reading the usual historical background sources.[10]

His conception shows a friendlier Whitelaw Reid and a good-humored Mergenthaler seated at his machine, enjoying his part in the historic event. Through the window can be seen the City Hall cupola, across the street from the

Tribune building. Reid's hand on Mergenthaler's shoulder indicates informality and recognition, and makes DePol's version the warmest and most human of the three studies. Upon reading Mergenthaler's *Biography*, however, one might think the inventor would have seen the Wilson version as a closer personality portrayal of how Reid turned out to be. —CARL SCHLESINGER

NOTES:

1. Henry Hope Reed, *The New York Public Library, Its Architecture and Decoration* (New York: W.W. Norton and Company, 1986) Pages 126-7.
2. Ibid.
3. Adolph of Nassau, Elector of Mainz, was Gutenberg's only known benefactor, who granted Gutenberg a small pension in recognition of his work.
4. Interview with Mergenthaler's widow in the *Standard* newspaper of the St. Lawrence (Thousand Islands region), circa summer 1906.
5. Isaac Newton Phelps Stokes, a Library benefactor, furnished Laning's supplies. The murals were part of a government Works Progress Administration program for artists affected by the 1930's Depression.
6. Sean Jennett, *Pioneers in Printing* (London: Routledge & Kegan Paul Ltd., 1958) Page 170.
7. *Who Was Who in American Art* and *The American Art Annual.*
8. A brief history of Whitelaw Reid during the Linotype period is in Richard Kluger's book *The Paper* (New York: Alfred A. Knopf Company, 1986) Pages 149-153.
9. The Yellow Barn Press, Council Bluffs, Iowa, has published some recent DePol works.
10. Author's conversation with Mr. DePol, June 1988.

PART III

The Secret Matrices
That Ottmar Mergenthaler Used
To Cast the First Type
on His 1886 Linotype

and

Finding the First Linotyped Stories
Hidden in the July 3, 1886
New York Tribune

By
CARL SCHLESINGER

A FULL-SIZE REPRODUCTION OF THIS PAGE WILL BE FOUND IN A POCKET ON THE INSIDE BACK COVER

THE FIRST NEWSPAPER PAGE TO BE SET ON A LINOTYPE

The greater portion of this editorial page was composed on the first commercial Linotype placed in a Newspaper Plant. It revolutionized composing room methods and made possible the great Newspapers of today.

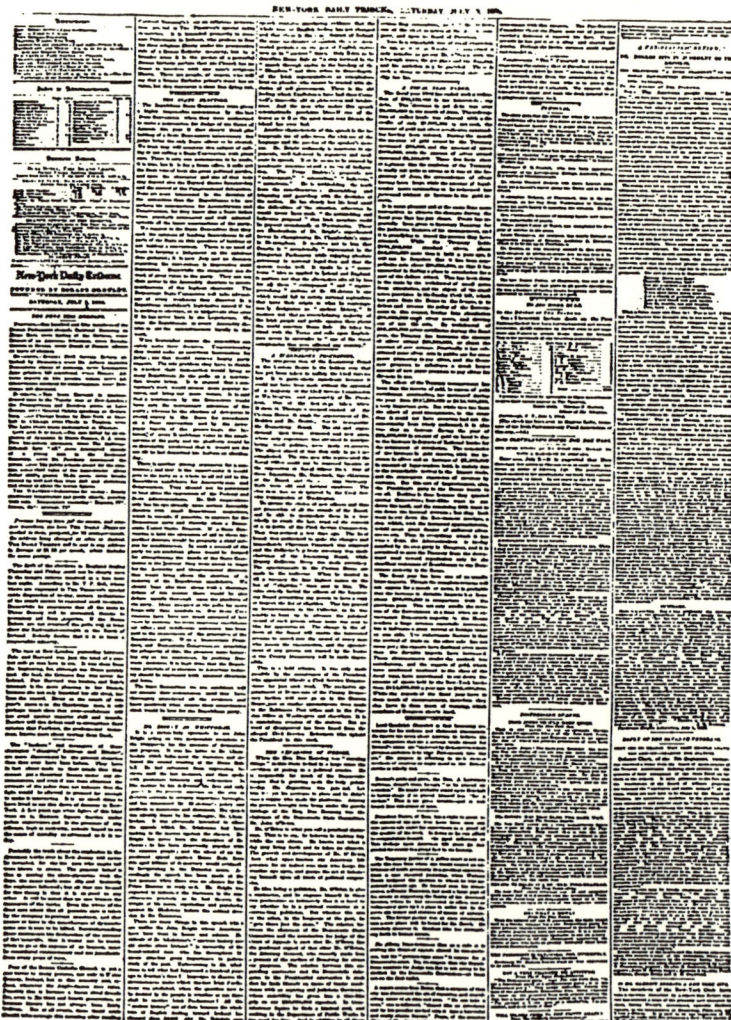

N. Y. Tribune Editorial Page, July 3, 1886

DURING the winter of 1886 inventor Ottmar Mergenthaler faced a major problem posed by his principal backer, publisher Whitelaw Reid of the *New York Tribune*. Reid wanted Mergenthaler's new typesetting machine to produce type that looked exactly like the typeface that the *Tribune* was already using in its newspaper.

Wanting to please the publisher, the inventor agreed to the idea, only to find he was up against one of the more difficult challenges of his career. Making new type in the exact image of someone else's design was simply not possible, that is, if one relied on the traditional method of type creation that had been practiced for more than 400 years.

In that system, highly skilled punchcutters, who were both artists and engravers, designed and then cut a master type face into the tops of short steel bars, called punches. They worked painstakingly by hand, under magnifying glasses, first scratching the letter design in reverse into the steel and then cutting it in relief with tiny files and gravers. (See Page 107 and Fig. 1, Page 108.)

As skilled as the traditional type engravers were, they could not cut exact copies of someone else's typeface, especially in the very small sizes. Each engraver's individuality meant that the copied face would be slightly different from the original, especially when the two faces were viewed together.

Mergenthaler did make a successful, matching typeface, however. He used a different process, called electroplating. In this electro-chemical method, the inventor made a copper shell of each of the *Tribune's* hand types that he wished to duplicate. Then he soldered those tiny shells of the copied type design into his circulating matrices, which he used in his machine. (A reconstruction of how he might have done this is in Fig. 6, page 111.)

These special matrices were used to cast the first live Linotype slugs for part of the *New York Tribune's* edition of July 3, 1886. The electrotyped mats were also used to set the main text for the first Linotyped book, *The Tribune Book of Open-Air Sports,* published at the end of 1886.

In his *Biography,* on page 29, Mergenthaler describes the difficulties he ran into trying to manufacture his single circulating matrices, which system is the heart of his typesetting machine. (See diagram, Page 118.) He writes nothing, however, about the electrotyping process he used and the secret matrices he made to meet and conquer the challenge posed by Reid's requirement. In fact, there is no record in any of the inventor's surviving papers about this important event. Perhaps that is why no one has written about it, or indicated they were aware of it, for more than 100 years.

Using recently discovered letters from the Whitelaw Reid papers collection in the Library of Congress, plus other evidence and researched conjecture, I offer proof that the process was used during the crucial six-month period of March to August 1886, when the first live types were cast on the Linotype. The electrotype matrices were not only used but they succeeded so well that not even the Linotype Company seemed to know where the Linotype slugs had been placed to blend in alongside the copied hand type.

The following information is offered to support my hypothesis.

The composing room foreman of the *Tribune,* G.L. Thompson, was the technical supervisor responsible to Publisher Reid for the typographical appearance of the paper. While the first production model of the "Blower" typesetter was being built, (the machine was called that because blasts of air were used to "blow" the matrices into position), Foreman Thompson visited Mergenthaler at the inventor's Baltimore factory.

In a letter to Reid dated March 24, 1886, Thompson wrote

> We put in type [cast some slugs from the machine] several articles which, with your permission, will be printed in the Tribune. I should have remained longer, but the face of type is not *ours* & do not think it would look well printed in this paper with our type. This however I have compared, and no other reading need appear on the 6th page the day it is printed. They are constructing a machine with *our* face.
>
> A workman told our Mr. White that some remarkable improvements are coming, they propose to make a series of steel matrices...

I have found no evidence of the use of Linotype in the *Tribune* before July 3, 1886. It is possible that Reid did not give permission for this experiment, deciding to wait instead for the matching typeface to be completed.

The electroplating of type for making matrices at the factory had started before Thompson's letter was written. Reid himself was already aware of what was going on, though Mergenthaler may have kept the details from Thompson. In another letter discovered in the Reid papers is a note from Publisher Reid to M.W. Johnson, who was supervising Mergenthaler's Camden Street factory in Baltimore. Dated March 7, 1886, Reid writes enthusiastically:

> I am extremely glad to learn that the process of electrotyping matrices for the type has at last begun. Please let me know whether [ ] will be different sizes and characters have been used, and if not, precisely what sizes of type and what characters are now in the electrotyping bath.
>
> I am anxious about this because it is more important at the outset to get the smaller sizes, nonpareil and agate, than the larger ones.

Though Reid seemed to want all the *Tribune's* typefaces to be duplicated, in fact only the brevier (equivalent to an 8 point modern size) seems to have actually been made into the electrotyped form and appeared in the paper. The reason was that the process foundered after a while on the reactions of differing metals, i.e., copper shell soldered into steel or brass matrices, subjected to wear of machine circulation, casting of molten lead at high temperatures, breaking down of thin sidewalls of the matrices, and just normal wearing out.

By August 10th, a little more than a month after the first successful demonstration using the electrotyped matrices, Reid's administrative assistant, Ernest Lambert, telegraphed the publisher at his father-in-law's Millbrae, California ranch:

> MERGENTHALER EXPECTS FINISH MINION [equal to 7 point modern type size] 21ST. [.] CANNOT FINISH OTHER BEFORE TESTING THE NONPAREIL [equal to 6 point] BEFORE SEPT. FIRST ... MERGENTHALER STOP[PED] ELECTROTYPING MATRICES SAYING THEY DON'T STAND.

A portion of Reid's letter to Johnson and the above telegram are shown in Fig. 8 on page 112.

Lambert wrote further to Reid the next day:

> I enclose a partial report from Mr. Thompson [composing room foreman] by which you will see he now attributes the blurring to the wearing of the copper on the matrix, which exposes the body. He thinks that this will be overcome now that they are punching the matrices in solid brass, like the sample sent you herewith. It is intended to complete the whole font of brevier [8 point modern size] in this way ... Mr. Hine [executive of the Mergenthaler Company] has just given [James] West the punch cutter the contract to make all the punches the company will need for one year.

Though Mergenthaler seems to have put nothing in writing about the electrotypes, he did make a sketch of a matrix which contained an "eye" where an electrotype insert could be placed. The sketch is on Page 23 of his *Biography,* alongside the drawing of his 1885 first circulating-matrix machine which preceded the "Blower" model.

There is one other passing mention of the process. On pages 90-91, in the May 19, 1889 article that describes the problems of the Linotype's first years of operation, the unnamed writer of the article notes:

> But perhaps the most troublesome experience of all was with the matrices. The moulds for these were at first electrotyped from ordinary type but after repeated casting, the electrotyped deposit pulled off and left them useless.

Not so useless, really, because for six months, from March to August 1886, these unique matrices evidently satisfied Reid and saved the day for Mergenthaler in the "matching typeface test" at the *Tribune.* They were another of Mergenthaler's ingenious inventions, and the newspaper stories and the book they produced bear witness to their practicality.

Why Mergenthaler never mentioned the mats' existence is open to speculation. Electrotyping was used extensively in the 1880's by some manufacturers of hand type. They employed the process sometimes to save having to make duplicate punches for their type when a punch broke or wore out. They also used it to "appropriate" popular designs from another manufacturer without permission, skirting or ignoring what weak copyright laws then existed for typeface protection.

By keeping his method secret perhaps Mergenthaler avoided being accused of this kind of design pirating. The inventor knew there was already much suspicion of the profound effect his typesetting machine might have on the economics of the hand-type manufacturing industry. Because the matrices wore out prematurely, perhaps he was also reluctant to write about one of his less-than-completely-successful ideas.

In 1987 I was fortunate enough to inspect samples of electrotyped matrices of recent vintage, custom-made for the Linotype, owned by printer Norman Cordes of Glen Rock, New Jersey. They provided positive proof that the process could work. A photo of one matrix appears in Fig. 7, page 112.

Though none of Mergenthaler's electrotyped matrices have been located, in my opinion their existence now seems unquestionable.

Just how good was the type produced by these matrices? Did their design really blend in with the *Tribune's* hand-set typeface? The answer is Yes. The match was good enough to fool the readers and most printers. How the lines were found, and how that led to discovering what process the inventor used, is discussed in the second part of this article, on page 113.

Some further details on the making and use of type punches

One steel punch was made for each letter of the alphabet, capital and lower case, and small capitals where called for. Others were made for each number, punctuation mark, accent and special characters. As many as 90 punches were needed for a basic set of characters in one size and style of type.

Once the punch was completed, the steel was hardened further. Then the end with the type design on it was struck into a flat bar of softer copper. The resulting sunken image in the copper, called a "strike," was then aligned to form a matrix. (See Fig. 2, page 109.)

The matrix was locked at the bottom of a steel box-like mold, into which molten lead was poured. The matrix's design-image left its impression, reversed, on the piece of hardening lead. The mold was opened and the hardened lead, now a piece of hand type, was taken out. (See Fig. 3, page 109.)

The Operating Principle of the Linotype

In Mergenthaler's typesetting machine no individual pieces of type were made or used. Instead, many matrices (See Fig. 4, page 110), made from brass or (possibly in the beginning) soft steel, were stored in the machine and circulated continuously through the mechanism. The matrices were assembled into words and sentences by a keyboard operator. When a line of predetermined length was full, the mats were sent to another part of the machine, where the face of the matrices was pressed against a casting mold.

Molten lead was squirted into the mold, which was shaped like a long thin bar. As the lead hardened (almost immediately), it picked up the type design of the assembled matrices, in a reversed image, on the bar. These type characters would then stand out in relief, about 1/32d of an inch high, on the edge of the newly cast type bar. (See Fig. 5, page 110.)

The printing bar was automatically pushed out of the machine and onto a steel tray, called a galley, alongside the machine operator. The bar then became one of the "lines of type" in the story being composed.

While the lead bar was being pushed out, Mergenthaler's ingenious machine was automatically disassembling the matrices and spaces from their word groups. By means of a worm screw and a "code" cut into metal teeth at the top of each matrix, the machine was able to return each mat to its storage area, ready to be used again to form new words. (See picture, page 118.)

The inventor needed 1200 matrices (multiple amounts of each letter, etc., all of the same face and size), to stock just one of his machines. He thought they could be made for six cents each. Imagine his reaction when he was told by a type foundry they could not be made for less than a dollar each. He then invented thirty of his own machines and tools to make his own matrices.

FIG. 1. The late Harry Carter, English punchcutter, is shown at his bench at the Oxford University Press Printing House, cutting a letter design on the end of a steel bar. The skill requires the eye of a lettering artist, the super-steady hands of an engraver, knowledge of metallurgy, of type and legibility, and great patience. One letter or character is cut on each bar, using tiny cutting gravers and files. Sometimes steel "counter-punches" are made to clear the space inside an "O," "g," "B" or other letters. In cutting an alphabet the engraver first scratches his design, in reverse, on the end of the steel bar. Each character must have the same design characteristics to make a complete matching font.

A font can require 90 or more punches: 26 capitals, 26 lower case letters, 26 small capitals, 10 numbers and 10 or more special characters. A candle is used to make "smoke proofs" to check the progress of each punch as the work progresses. The finished punch is a unique expression of the punchcutter's personal skill. When a punch breaks, its hand-cut replacement will never be an exact twin.

Reproducible punches came with the invention of the Benton punch cutter machine in 1884, by Linn Boyd Benton in Milwaukee, Wisconsin. Philip Dodge, patent lawyer for the Linotype Company, bought some of the machines in 1889 and Linotype began using the equipment then. It saved the company from foundering, because at that point Linotype could not produce hand-cut steel punches or make matrices fast enough to stock the typesetters as they were being built.

FIG. 2. At left, the soft copper matrix bar (A) carries a sunken impression of a letter after it has been struck by the hardened steel punch (B).

At right: A similar punch-strike method is the normal process used to make the many brass matrices used in the Linotype. Except for Mergenthaler's electrotyped matrices, the method shown here (in very simplified form) began in 1886 and continues to the present.

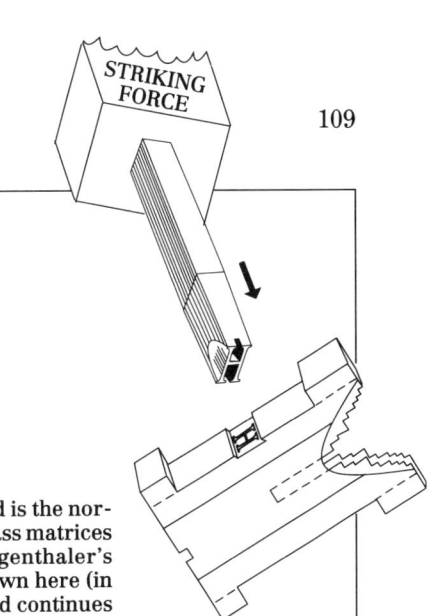

A punched Linotype matrix (made of brass).

FIG. 3. Below: Casting a piece of hand type using a mold and a copper matrix bar. Molten lead (A) is poured into the mold (B). At the bottom of the mold the copper matrix (C) has been locked in to give the type its "face.") The type is cast upside down. At lower right, a finished, single piece of hand type shows the reverse impression of the matrix design, on top of a squared-off lead body. Casting of hand type in the Western World began in the 1440's, developed by Johann Gutenberg, first printer, of Mainz, Germany.

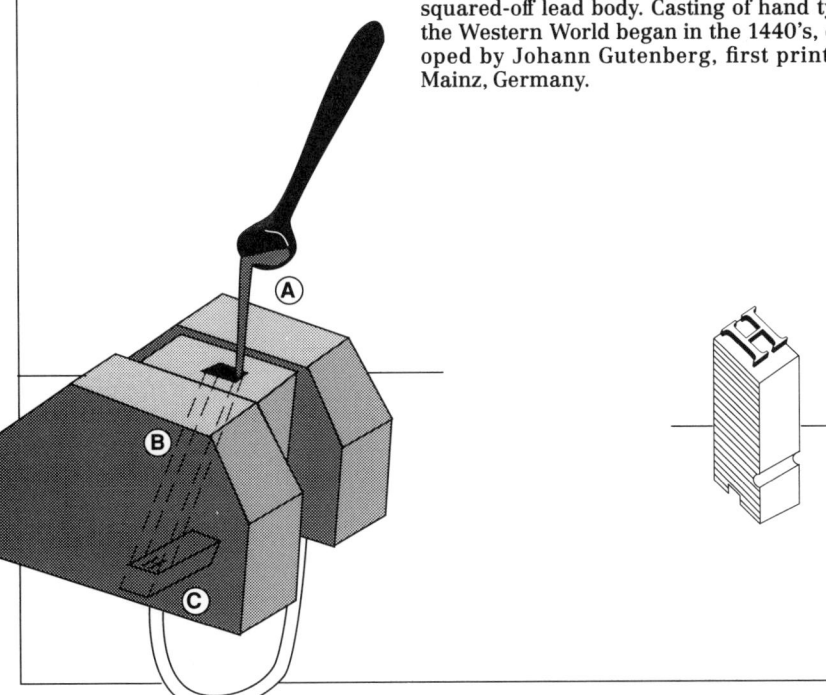

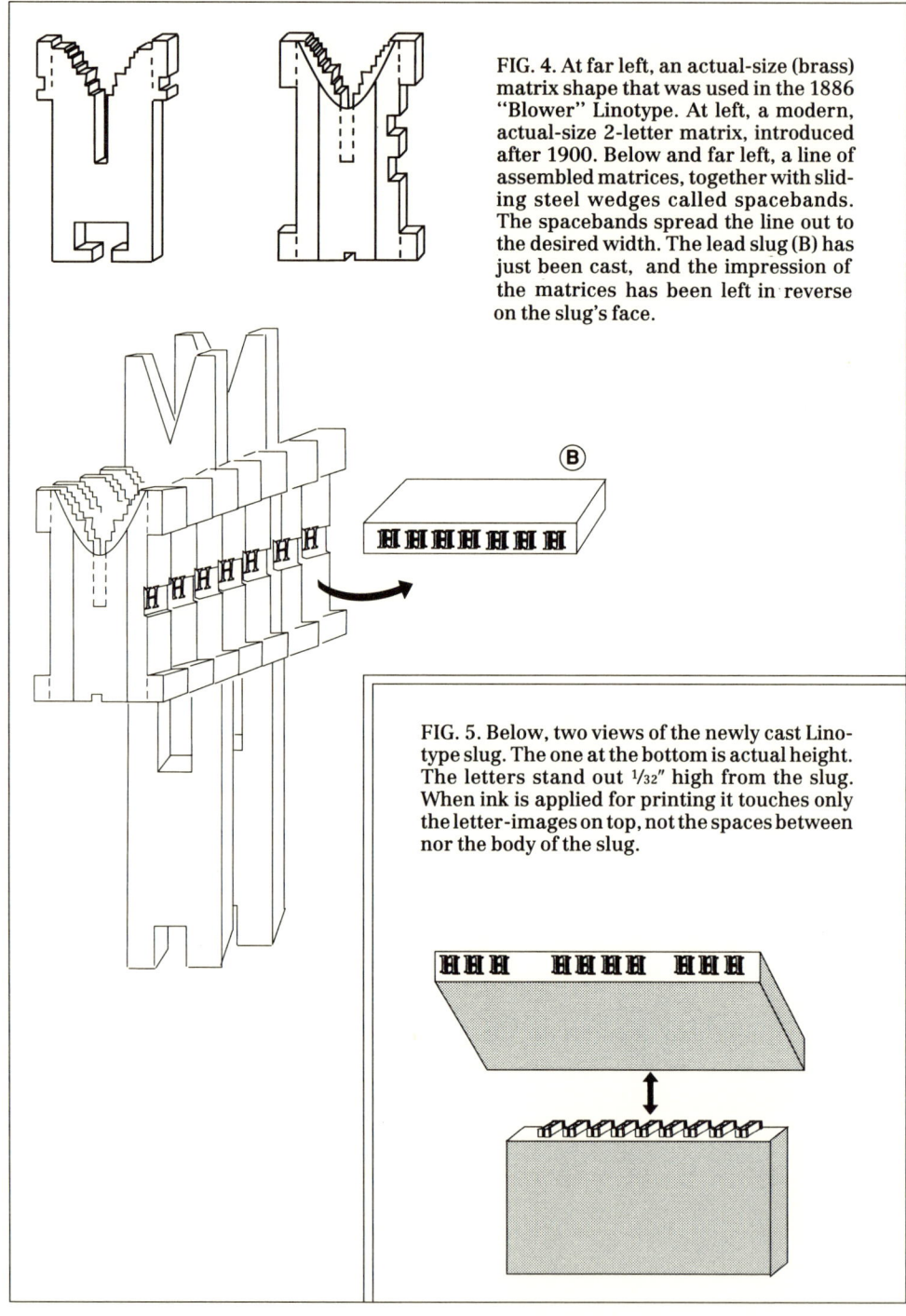

FIG. 4. At far left, an actual-size (brass) matrix shape that was used in the 1886 "Blower" Linotype. At left, a modern, actual-size 2-letter matrix, introduced after 1900. Below and far left, a line of assembled matrices, together with sliding steel wedges called spacebands. The spacebands spread the line out to the desired width. The lead slug (B) has just been cast, and the impression of the matrices has been left in reverse on the slug's face.

FIG. 5. Below, two views of the newly cast Linotype slug. The one at the bottom is actual height. The letters stand out 1/32″ high from the slug. When ink is applied for printing it touches only the letter-images on top, not the spaces between nor the body of the slug.

How Mergenthaler's Copper Electrotyped Shells Could Have Been Made
(A Reconstruction Theory)

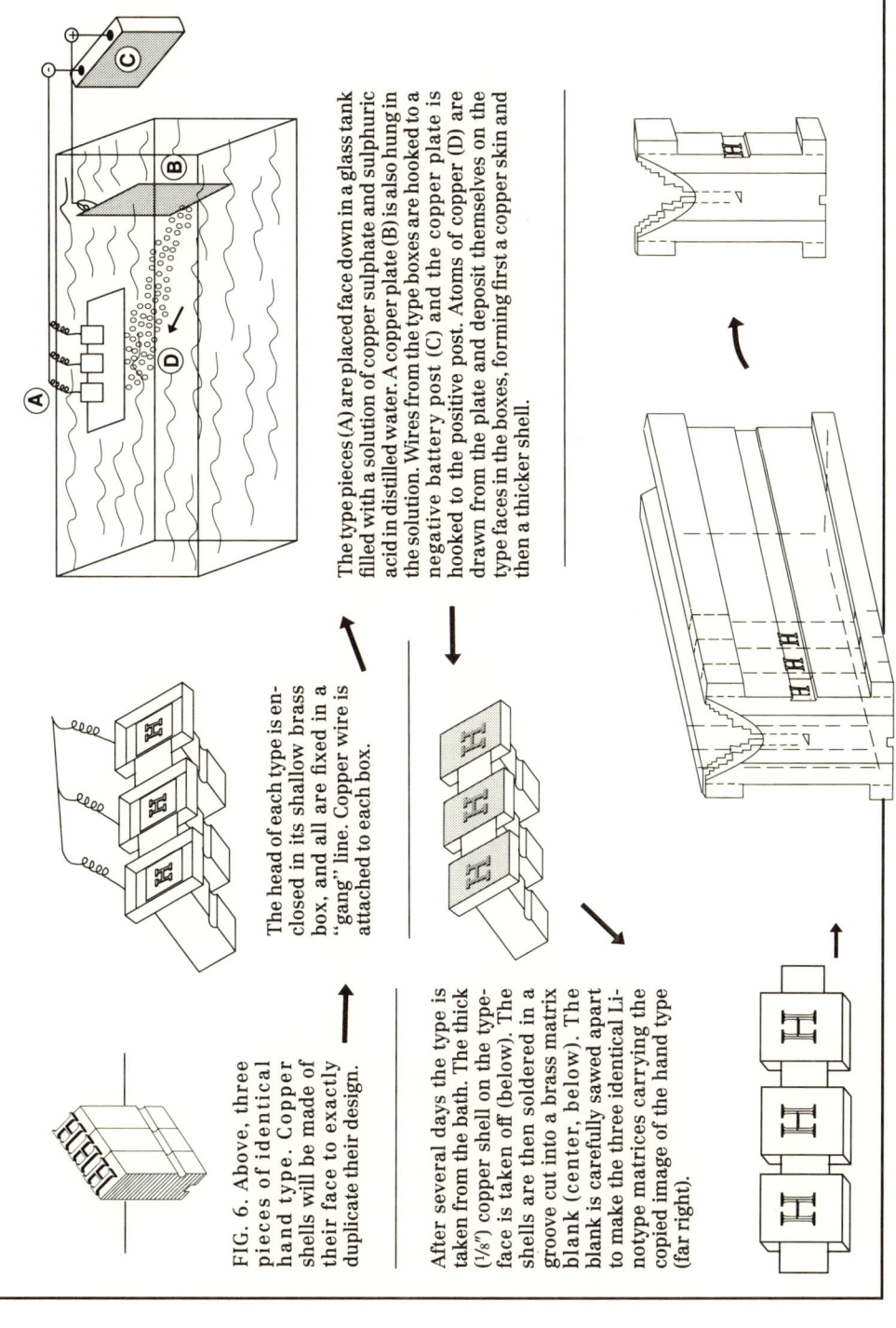

FIG. 6. Above, three pieces of identical hand type. Copper shells will be made of their face to exactly duplicate their design.

The head of each type is enclosed in its shallow brass box, and all are fixed in a "gang" line. Copper wire is attached to each box.

The type pieces (A) are placed face down in a glass tank filled with a solution of copper sulphate and sulphuric acid in distilled water. A copper plate (B) is also hung in the solution. Wires from the type boxes are hooked to a negative battery post (C) and the copper plate is hooked to the positive post. Atoms of copper (D) are drawn from the plate and deposit themselves on the type faces in the boxes, forming first a copper skin and then a thicker shell.

After several days the type is taken from the bath. The thick (1/8") copper shell on the typeface is taken off (below). The shells are then soldered in a groove cut into a brass matrix blank (center, below). The blank is carefully sawed apart to make the three identical Linotype matrices carrying the copied image of the hand type (far right).

FIG. 7. Two views of custom-made electrotype matrices, of recent vintage. Copper shells were made of special hand-type characters that the printer wished to copy for use in his Linotype. The electrodeposited copper shell was then inset into a matrix (see arrow). A dovetail groove was made to keep the shell from pulling out of the matrix.

Sample of special characters Ⓦ Ⓧ Ⓨ Ⓩ

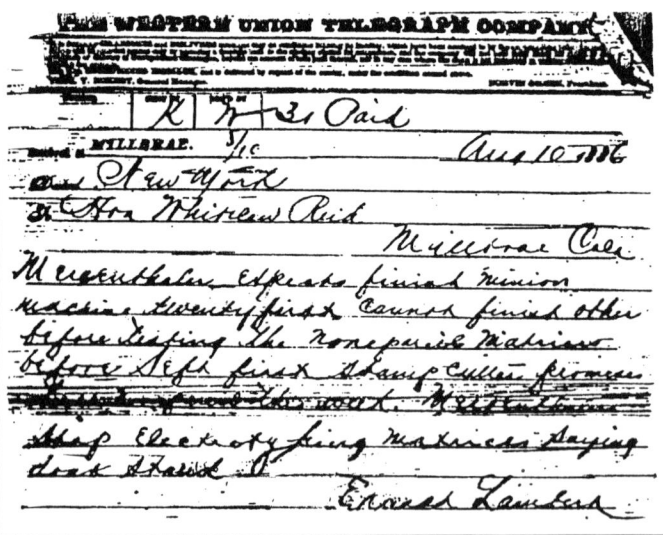

FIG. 8. Above: part of the letter from Whitelaw Reid to M.W. Johnson of Mergenthaler's Baltimore factory, written March 7, 1886, that acknowledges the beginning of the electrotype process. Left: Telegram to Whitelaw Reid on Aug. 10, 1886 sent by assistant Ernest Lambert, telling of Mergenthaler's decision to stop electrotyping of matrices.

Finding the Linotyped Stories
In the July 3, 1886 New York Tribune

THE year 1986 was the 100th anniversary of the first use of the Linotype typesetter at the *New York Tribune.* Early in that year I was fortunate to be able to read Corban Goble's excellent doctoral dissertation, *Obituary of a Machine: The rise and fall of Ottmar Mergenthaler's Linotype at U.S. newspapers.*[1] Goble includes in his work a reduced-size photo of the first page to contain Linotype printing bars. (See page 102.) He found this promotional material in the Mergenthaler family papers. A caption on top of the sheet, separated from the news matter, reads:

> SET ON A LINOTYPE. The greater portion of this editorial page was composed on the first commercial Linotype placed in a Newspaper Plant. It revolutionized composing methods and made possible the great newspapers of today.[2]

Goble added his own comments about the machine's use at the *Tribune* when he wrote:

> Tradition has it that type from the first Mergenthaler [Blower machine] was used for portions of the Tribune editorial page of 3 July 1886. The page does not appear markedly different from others of that time. No mention of the conversion to a new composition style appeared on that date.[3]

I own an original issue of that *Tribune* newspaper, but I confess to not inspecting it carefully until that day. Goble's remarks on the lack of distinguishing features of the Linotype lines made me curious.

I opened my copy to the Page 4 editorial page and scanned it, feeling sure that after 40 years of printing experience, and as a former Linotype operator, I would quickly spot the famous lines.

It was not so. An assortment of type sizes was scattered over the page, but nothing unique or different was immediately apparent. To me, that was quite alarming.

As a serious student of printing history, how could I determine that there really *were* Linotype lines on that page? A promotional reprint that hints the lines are there somewhere should not be enough to satisfy me, nor would it satisfy the printing scholars of tomorrow. In the many articles, books and official company histories I had read, I could not remember any discussion of those lines or even mention of them.

The more I thought about this the more I became determined to solve the mystery. To help the reader follow my line of reasoning there is included in the back of this book a full-size reproduction of the page in question.

At first glance there was nothing unusual about the type faces on the page, so how was one to know where to start? Neither historians Goble, Huss or others provide any new clues in their writings when they quote letters from Mergenthaler discussing the making of type sizes.[4] The documents they quote indicated that the type faces of minion, brevier, nonpareil and agate (modern 8, 7, 6 and 5 1/2 point type, respectively) had not yet been made into Linotype matrices as late as mid-August 1886.

Since all these faces were also shown on the July 3d page, just where *was* the Linotype to be found?

I started my close inspection with a premise: Type used on the page, if it were hand-composed, would show signs of wear, since it was re-used each day. Some letters should show battered corners from being dropped back into the type case during redistribution. Linotype, on the other hand, should show sharp and clear edges, since the lines were cast new every day.

My theory held up. Under a magnifying glass the type faces of minion, agate and pearl all showed noticeable uniform wear and battering, particularly the "g" descenders, serifs on "n"'s, sides of "o"'s, and also some capitals.

The same condition held for the italic faces, which were mostly minion in size; capitals showed wear and battering. My first inspection, then, eliminated from further consideration all the type but the brevier (8-point editorial matter). The brevier was spaced out, making it easier to inspect each line.

I examined the brevier type story by story. In column 1, at the left, starting under the italic in the middle of the page, there was uniform wear of the letters. Then, in the third paragraph down, line 4, I saw a mark between the words "ever" and "have" which seemed to be a high space—a piece of spacing type that did not settle to the bottom of the line as it should have.

Spaces, being shorter than letters, are not supposed to print. When they do it indicates that the article was composed in hand type, where each piece can move individually. A space in a loosely justified line can be pulled up to type height by the sticky ink used when proofing a page. This is particularly true in newspaper typography, where spaces are higher than found in commercial letterpress printing, as they must bear off the weight when a stereotyper's mat is pressed against them. The space must have moved up and then been locked into the high position when the newspaper page form went under the stereotyper's press. (The stereotyper's cardboard matrix that resulted was then used to make a semicircular lead plate for rotary printing presses.)

Linotype spaces between words cannot work up and print, since they are cast into the solid metal bar.

The top story in Column 2, headed "The State Election," proved to be more hand composition. In addition to battered letters, there were four more high spaces, with the first one being in the opening paragraph of the story.[5]

The editorial at the bottom of Column 2, "Mr. Bright as Whipper-In," was something else again. Though the face was the same as the hand-composed story above it, the type letters were sharper and clearer. There were no high spaces. The type face showed tiny breaks in many of the letters, resulting in a lighter overall tone for the story. The lighter impression of the letters could have come from various problems: uneven metal temperature when the face was cast, or because the face was new it would be slightly lighter than the surrounding worn hand type. At the time it didn't occur to me that the breaks could also have come from electrotyped matrices that were wearing thin.

There were no high spaces showing. *This could be the Linotype.*

The next two stories, in columns 3 and 4, also had type that was sharp and clear and contained no high spaces.[6] On further inspection, all three of these suspected Linotype articles had another peculiarity: a bold-face punctuation character that repeated itself regularly.

This single wrong-font apostrophe turned up as part of a close of quotation, or before an "s" that showed possession, or in a contraction.

It started occurring at the bottom of Column 2, in the 13th line of the editorial "Mr. Bright as Whipper-In": "...Gladstone's policy..." Then the character occurred again in closing quotes in Column 3, starting with the sixth line ("ancient") and ninth line ("Kingdom"), and continued to appear at intervals through the next two editorials.

This peculiarity is not found in any of the hand-set matter. I feel this matrix was a wrong-font letter that escaped detection when the typeface was being electroplated. It was discovered too late to re-make the character in time for the July 3d typesetting. The matrix was stored in the Linotype and recirculated. As it was needed, it fell into composed lines at random places.

The last story set in brevier type is in Column 4: "A Fiscal Year Ended." As I inspected it under a magnifier, I found that suddenly we were back to hand-set type. The typeface design is still identical, but now the letters show definite signs of wear and battering. The second line of the story, beginning with the suffix "tion," has a battered "o". On line 6 we find a battered figure "0" in the "1,000,000" figures. On line 7 there is a battered "v" in "silver," all signs of worn hand type.

My conclusion is that the three editorial stories: "Mr. Bright as Whipper-In," "A Scandalous Proceeding" and "The Expansion of O'Brien" **were the first stories to be set by Linotype and to appear in any commercial newspaper.**

The type was an identical match to the hand-type that surrounded it—a severe test of Mergenthaler's electrotype process and one that his matrices and machine passed very well.

I feel the lines on the *Tribune* page that were set by Linotype have now been identified. Again, my thanks go to Corban Goble, whose remarks in his dissertation started my search. We can now see another dimension added to the technological obstacles that Mergenthaler had to overcome in his efforts to please his main backer, Whitelaw Reid, while at the same time trying to build a practical typesetting machine for the whole printing industry.

Once the Linotype was identified, the next question was "How could Mergenthaler have done such a perfect type-matching job?" Knowing something of the difficulty of cutting type designs on punches[7], I marveled at Mergenthaler's imitation. Since he had left no written clues, however, I worked my way through several theories during the years 1986-1988. One day I discovered Reid's letter to Johnson (page 104) and then Lambert's telegram to Reid (page 105) indicating the beginning and end of the electrotyping process, buried in the Whitelaw Reid papers at the Library of Congress. After further research[8] I offer this paper to support my conclusions.

The First Linotyped Book

About the same time as the first newspaper articles appeared, the *Tribune* decided to use the Linotype to compose a book. The 500-page volume was a premium to promote circulation for the newspaper. Charles Letsch, the machinist who installed the first *Tribune* typesetter, said that

> The first Linotype in that office was run during the day on a wide measure slug to get out a premium book called *The Tribune Book of Open-Air Sports,* and every evening it was changed to set type for the regular newspaper size—which change...took more than an hour every time.[9]

Since only the one Linotype was at the *Tribune* in early July 1886, and since only the electrotyped matrices were ready for use at that time, it is logical that the book would also have been set using the electrotyped matrices.

When I examined the reading text in an original book I found this to be true. The brevier face in the book is the exact type face used to set the editorial matter in the newspaper. The type is sharp and clear, and has the same slightly broken characteristic of the newspaper Linotype. The wrong font apostrophe was not found, but it probably had been removed when the book was begun.

Aside from the hand type used on the book's title page, (Fig. 9, page 120), the other main type face used was an agate (5 1/2 point) size, for statistical tables. This type may have been set from conventional punched matrices, for the agate face was available by October of 1886.[10] (See Fig. 11, page 121.)

The inscription on the reverse side of the book's title page, reproduced as Fig. 10, page 120, notes that the book was printed "Without Type," meaning of course without hand-set type. But the face for that announcement resembles a copperplate gothic style, with its large and small capitals. There is no proof that this face was cut for machine matrices in the early years, as it does not show up in the 1888 Linotype specimen sheet inspected by me at the Linotype Company archives.

What irony it would be if these lines, announcing the historic change to typesetting by machine, were themselves composed in hand-set letters!

NOTES

1. George Corban Goble, *Obituary of a Machine: The rise and fall of Ottmar Mergenthaler's Linotype at U.S. newspapers* (Ann Arbor, MI: University Microfilm International, 1984).
2. Page 437, ibid.
3. Page 80, ibid.
4. In 1987, while examining some of the Whitelaw Reid papers at the Library of Congress, I saw Mergenthaler's Sept. 11, 1886 letter to Reid, in which he writes "...the first minion machine is far enough advanced to commence a test by Monday noon. The steel type [punches] for nonpareil are done and Mr. West is just starting on the agate. He cannot get them done within a month...The machines now going on are minion and nonpareil..." We see proof that none of these faces were ready on the July 3, 1886 date. Ernest Lambert, Reid's representative, had written to Reid (August 10) that the brevier (8 point size) was still being worked on. I conclude that *none* of the punched fonts were ready on July 3d. Only Mergenthaler's unmentioned, special electrotype matrices were available.
5. Some of the high "spaces" might be upside-down thin letters like "i" or "l," which were distributed back into the spaces box by mistake, and picked up again by the compositor, thinking they were spaces, as he was quickly setting his lines. I assume this because the black squares seen on the newspaper page resemble the inked feet of a piece of hand type.
6. A puzzling exception is the Column 3 article "A Scandalous Proceeding." In line 6, between the first two words "of a" appears what could be a smudge that looks like a high space. Since I believe that line to be Linotype, perhaps it is a piece of dirt that was in the space area when the page was stereotyped or a defect in the cardboard matrix which found its way to the printed page.
7. Several sources are recommended to the reader: the 45-minute videotape, *From Punch to Printing Type,* shows Stan Nelson, a Museum Specialist in the Division of Graphic Arts of the Smithsonian Institution, actually cutting punches. Available from Book Arts Press Production, School of Library Service, Columbia University, New York, NY 10027. For a wider historical overview of punchcutting, the videotape *The World of Letterforms* (St. Paul, MN: Purup Electronics North America, 1986). Also, article by Edward Pye on "Typefounding," *A Typographical Journey Through the Inland Printer:* (Baltimore, Md., Maran Press, 1977) pp. 66-68, and Richard E. Huss's fine book, *The Printer's Composition Matrix* (New Castle, DE: Oak Knoll Books, 1985) pp. 3-6.
8. Huss, pp. 28-29. *Inland Printer* (compiled by Maurice Annenberg), p. 226. Lucien Legros, and John C. Grant, *Typographical Printing Surfaces* (London: Longmans, Green and Co., 1916.) pp. 238-9. Roy Rice, *Matrix Making at the Oxford University Press* (Atlanta, GA: The Recalcitrant Press, 1982.)
    Also, Theo Rehak, *Chapter 3, The Electro* (unpublished ms.): (Southard, Howell, NJ, The Benton Engraving Co, 1988.) Also, Patricia Knittel Cost, (unpublished masters thesis): (*Contributions of Linn Boyd Benton and Morris Fuller Benton to the Technology of Typesetting and Typeface Design* (Rochester Inst. of Technology, Rochester, NY, 1986) pages 19-44.
9. Interview with Letsch in *Linotype News* (company magazine), Aug. 1936, p.3.
10. A specimen proof of type from the agate matrices was found in the Whitelaw Reid letters. It was sent from Baltimore by Ernest Lambert, to Reid, on Aug. 11, 1886.

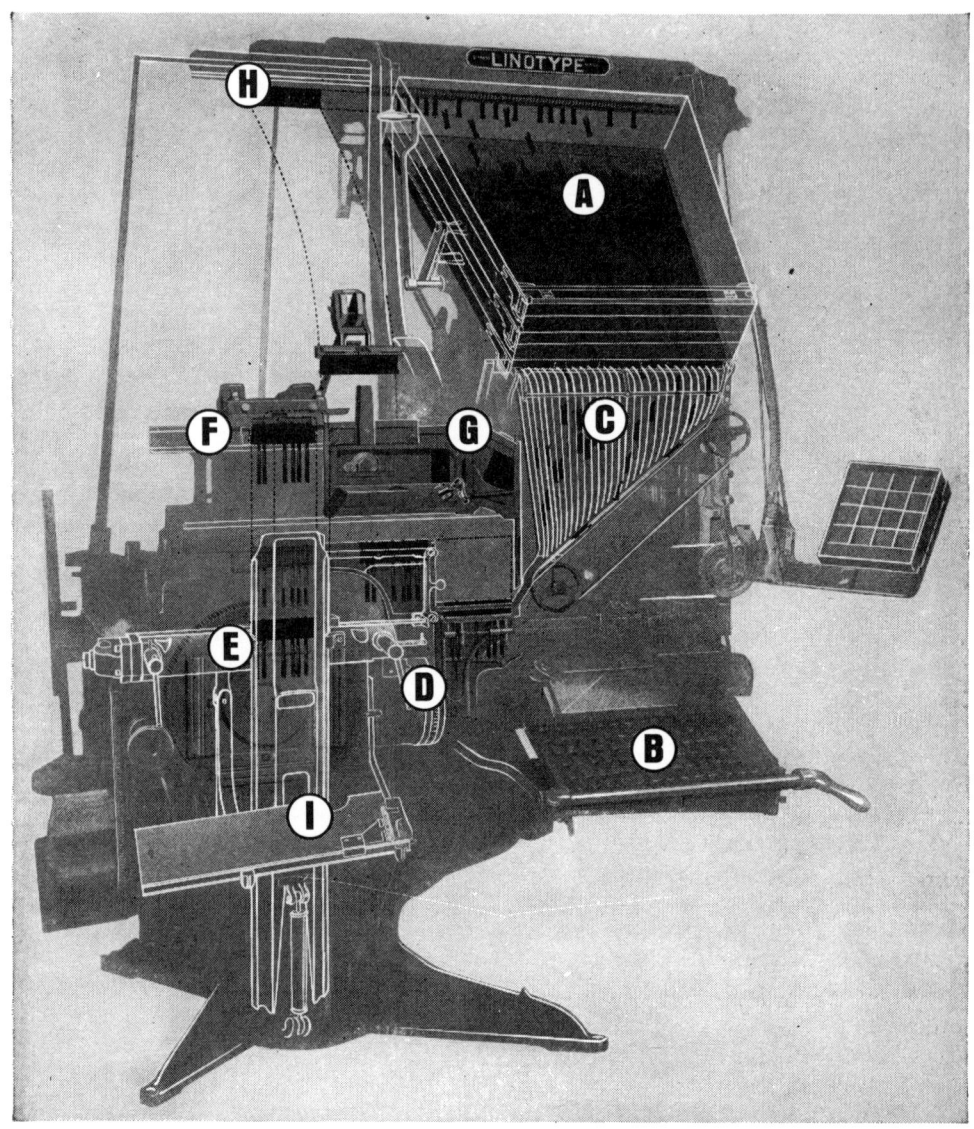

This illustration from the Linotype Company, called the "phantom" Linotype, illustrates the circulation of the type matrices through the machine.

Matrices are stored in the magazine (A). When a key is touched on the keyboard (B) the corresponding matrix is released from the magazine and falls down the gravity chute (C) and into the assembler (D).

When the operator has assembled a full line of matrices and spacebands he transfers them to the casting mechanism (E). Here the molten lead is pumped against the matrices' face and a Linotype slug is made. The matrice line then rises to (F), where spacebands are automatically pushed to their storage area (G) and the matrices are transferred to a second elevator. This carries them to the roof of the machine (H).

At that point the line of matrices is disassembled, and a worm screw rod slides each matrix along a slotted rail behind the magazine. Each matrix carries its own notched code. When the notched code coincides with the matching break in the slotted rail, the mat is released and automatically drops back into the magazine at its storage spot.

At point (I), the still-warm Linotype slug is ejected from the machine onto a steel galley tray, and becomes a line of type in a story.

> A FULL SIZE COPY OF THE NEW YORK TRIBUNE PAGE DESCRIBED HERE
> WILL BE FOUND IN A POCKET AT THE BACK OF THIS BOOK.

TABLE 1. Description of types used on Page 4 of July 3, 1886 issue.*

COL. 1: First 1½": Listing of Amusements (theaters, etc.), set in *nonpareil* (6-point equivalent) type.
  Next 1¼": Index of advertisements in the day's paper. Set in *pearl* (5-point equivalent) type.
  Next 2½": Small ads; subscription rates for the Tribune, and branch offices of the paper. Set in *agate* (5½-point equivalent) type.
  Next 4½": Summary of the day's news articles, and weather. Set in *minion* (7-point equivalent) type.
  Next 1": Business notice to subscribers. Set in italic but also contains roman small caps. Set in *brevier* (8-point equivalent) type.
BALANCE OF COL. 1, ALL OF COLS. 2, 3 AND THE FIRST 15½": OF COL. 4: All editorial matter, set in *brevier* and leaded approximately 2 points per line. Heads, set in italic caps of *minion*, separate each story.
BALANCE OF COL. 4: 7½": Short editorial comments, set in *minion* type.
COL. 5: First 1¼": Editorial comment continued, set in *minion* type.
BALANCE OF COL. 5: Editorial comment, insults to rival editors, readers' letters. Set in mixture of *pearl* and *nonpareil*.
COL. 6: Continuation of mixed text from Col. 5, set in *pearl* and *nonpareil*.

*Type face size verified using "The Instant Type Finder," an 8-power magnifier with an engraved lens showing heights of type letters from 4 to 14 point. (Henry Sherr Engravers, inventor, N.Y.C., 212-242-8630)

TABLE II. Point sizes of 1886 and their modern equivalents.

wood. The following alphabets show the different sizes up to great primer.

Diamond.... abcdefghijklmnopqrstuvwxyz
Pearl...... abcdefghijklmnopqrstuvwxyz
Agate...... abcdefghijklmnopqrstuvwxyz
Nonpareil... abcdefghijklmnopqrstuvwxyz
Minion..... abcdefghijklmnopqrstuvwxyz
Brevier .... abcdefghijklmnopqrstuvwxyz
Bourgeois ... abcdefghijklmnopqrstuvwxyz
Long primer . abcdefghijklmnopqrstuvwx
Small pica... abcdefghijklmnopqrstuv
Pica ...... abcdefghijklmnopqrst
English .... abcdefghijklmnopq
Great primer . abcdefghijklmn

The foregoing account is conformed to the designations made use of by American type-founders, but is substantially correct for England. *Agate*, however, is called *ruby*, in England, where, also, a size intermediate between nonpareil and minion is employed, called *emerald*.

The table shown at left is actual size and is taken from the 1889 edition of Webster's Unabridged Dictionary. The equivalent point* sizes are:

Diamond . . .4½pt. Bourgeois. . . 9 pt.
Pearl . . . . . . .5 pt. Long Primer .10 pt.
Agate . . . . .5½ pt. Small Pica. . .11 pt.
Nonpareil. . . .6 pt. Pica . . . . . . .12 pt.
Minion . . . . . .7 pt. English. . . . .14 pt.
Brevier. . . . . .8 pt. Great Primer 18 pt.

*1 point = 1/72d of an inch, in face height and width.

Above: Published as of January 1887, this 500-page Linotyped book was sold by the Tribune to boost its circulation. First of its kind, the book met a public need for an explanation in layman's language of the detailed rules for many sports and games. It also carried many recorded statistics.

FIG. 9. Below: The title page of the first Linotyped book. This page was set using hand type letters.

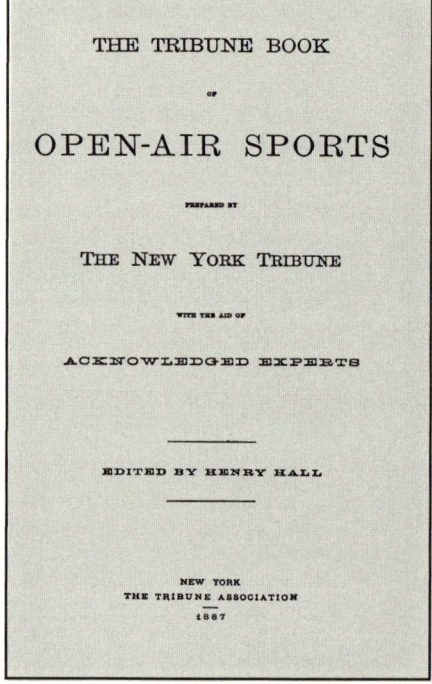

FIG. 10. Above: Reverse side of the title page. These two lines, set in tiny nonpareil capitals and small caps, announce to the world that an Industrial Revolution in typesetting was about to begin.

FIG. 11. A PAGE OF THE FIRST BOOK PRINTED FROM LINOTYPE SLUGS

BASE BALL. 101

club had been greatly strengthened this year for the race, and captured the pennant to their great joy. The Columbus and Louisville clubs also made a good fight and finished in second and third place respectively. The Washington and Indianapolis clubs were outclassed and brought up the rear. The success of the Metropolitan club was mainly due to the great pitching of Keefe and Lynch. The Metropolitans were given a rousing reception at the end of the season and a parade was organized in their honor. The parade was made at night and attracted considerable attention. The players were seated on the top of a tally ho coach and were loudly applauded all along the route. Many carriages and every amateur and semi-professional club in this vicinity followed the victorious baseball players. The clubs finished the season as follows.

Clubs.	Metropolitan	Columbus	Louisville	St. Louis	Cincinnati	Baltimore	Athletic	Toledo	Brooklyn	Virginia	Pittsburg	Indianapolis	Washington	Games Won	Games Played
Metropolitan		5	7	5	6	5	8	5	9	2	9	8	6	75	107
Columbus	4		5	7	4	5	8	7	2	9	8	5	5	69	108
Louisville	3	5		5	5	4	6	9	6	4	8	9	4	68	108
St. Louis	4	5	5		6	5	7	5	7	3	9	6	5	67	107
Cincinnati	4	3	5	4		6	4	7	8	4	8	9	6	68	109
Baltimore	5	6	6	5	4		3	5	5	5	9	9	2	63	106
Athletic	2	5	3	3	6	7		3	6	2	8	6	7	61	108
Toledo	4	1	1	5	3	5	3		4	4	5	6	5	46	104
Brooklyn	1	3	3	2	2	5	3	4		3	4	7	3	40	104
Virginia	0	2	1	1	0	0	0	0	2		4	2	0	12	43
Pittsburg	1	1	2	1	1	0	2	5	6	1		6	4	30	108
Indianapolis	2	2	1	3	1	1	2	3	3	1	4		4	29	107
Washington	2	1	1	1	0	1	1	1	1	0	1	2		12	63
Games Lost	32	39	40	40	41	43	47	58	64	31	78	78	51		

1885.

During the season of 1885 the Association recognized that the dozen club idea was a failure. All except eight of the clubs were dropped. Columbus, Toledo, Virginia, Indianapolis and Washington quietly withdrew. The struggle for the pennant this year was not so close as in previous seasons, the St. Louis Brown Stockings winning with ease. Their record was 79 victories out of 112 games played. The Metropolitans did wretchedly this year and finished seventh. Many people thought that when the manager left the club, taking with him pitcher Keefe and third baseman Esterbrook, he virtually took the backbone out of the Metropolitans. The Brooklyn club also did indifferently this season, and although it finished ahead of the "Indians," still it was far from the leader. The St. Louis club played a remarkably brilliant game all through the season and won the series from each of the other seven clubs. The glorious

Page 101 of *The Tribune Book of Open-Air Sports*. Actual size, set with brevier (8-point) electrotyped matrices and possibly with agate (5½-point) punched matrices for the tabular work.

BIBLIOGRAPHY

BOOKS

Annenberg, Maurice (Compiler). *A Typographical Journal Through The Inland Printer, 1883-1900* (Baltimore, MD, Maran Press, 1977).

Arnold, Edmund C. *Ink on Paper* (New York, Harper and Row, 1963).

Goble, Corban. *The Obituary of a Machine: Rise and Fall of Ottmar Mergenthaler's Linotype* (Ann Arbor, MI. University Microfilms Intl., 1985).

Huss, Richard E. *The Printer's Composition Matrix.* (New Castle, DE, Oak Knoll Books, 1985).

Jennett, Sean. *Pioneers in Printing* (London, Routledge & Kegan Paul Ltd., 1958).

Kelber, Harry and Carl Schlesinger. *Union Printers and Controlled Automation* (New York, Free Press, 1967).

Legros, Lucien A., and John Grant. *Typographical Printing Surfaces* (New York, Garland Publishing Company, reprint 1980 of the 1916 edition).

Levine, I.E. *Miracle Man of Printing–Ottmar Mergenthaler* (New York, Julian Messner, Inc. 1963).

Mengel, Willi. *Ottmar Mergenthaler and the Printing Revolution* (Brooklyn, Mergenthaler Linotype Company, 1954).

Romano, Frank. *Machine Writing and Typesetting (Story of Sholes and Mergenthaler)* (Salem, NH, GAMA, 1986).

Rosner, Charles. *Printer's Progress* (Cambridge, MA, Harvard University Press, 1951).

Smith, Anthony. *Goodbye Gutenberg* (New York, Oxford University Press, 1980).

Stevens, George, A. *History of New York Typographical Union No. 6* (Albany, NY, Dept. of Labor, 1913).

Thompson, John S. *Mechanism of the Linotype and History of Composing Machines.* (New York, Garland Publishing Co., reprint 1980 of 1902-04 edition).

ARTICLES

Bullen, Henry Lewis. "Origin and Development of the Linotype Machine," Inland Printer, Feb. and March 1924 issues.

Hicks, Clark B. "The Machine Comes to the Printing Industry," The Typographical Journal, CXI (July 1947), pp. 20-24.

Lawson, Alexander. "What the Composing Room Was Like 100 Years Ago," Inland Printer/Amer. Lithographer, CVLI (Dec. 1960).

Cost, Patricia. (Unpublished ms.) "Contributions of Linn Boyd Benton and Morris Fuller Benton to the Technology of Typesetting and Typeface Design." (Rochester, NY, R.I.T. School of Printing, 1986).

MERGENTHALER SOURCE MATERIALS

Library of Congress, Manuscript Division, Washington, DC (Whitelaw Reid Papers).
Linotype Company Archives, Hauppauge, NY.
Maryland Historical Society, Baltimore, MD.
National Museum of American History, Division of Graphic Arts, Washington, D.C.
University of Delaware Special Collections Library, Newark, DE.

INDEX FOR PART III

(Italic numbers indicate illustrations)

Agate type 114, 116, 117, *119*
Apostrophe, wrong font 115
Baltimore, Md 104
Benton, Linn Boyd 108
"Blower" typesetter 104, 110, 113
Brevier type 114, 115, *119*
Carter, Harry. *108*
Copper matrix bar 107, *109*
Copper shell 103, *111*
Copyright laws. 105
Cordes, Norman 106
Counter-punches. 108
Diamond type. *119*
Dodge, Philip 108
Electroplating 103, 104, *111*
Electrotyping, for matrices 104, 105, 106, *112*
English, type size *119*
First Newspaper Stories, by Linotype .115
Font. 108
Goble, Corban. 113, 115
Great primer, type size *119*
Gutenberg, Johann 109
Hand-set type 106, 107, *109, 111,* 114
Johnson, M.W.. . . . . .104, *112*
Lambert, Ernest. 105, *112*
Letsch, Charles. 116
Linotype, book. 116, *120, 121*
  Company 104, 108
  machine 103, 113, 114, *118*
  slug *110*, 115
Long primer, type size *119*

"Matching typeface test" 105
Matrices, circulating . . .103, 105, *110*, 116, *118*
  electrotype 111, *112*, 116, 117
  secret 103
Matrix 107, *109, 111*
Mergenthaler, Ottomar, Biography . .103, 105, 106, 115, 116
Minion, type size 105, 114, *119*
Molten lead. 107, *109*
Nonpareil, type size. . . .105, 114, 117, *119*
New York Tribune *102*, 103, 113, *119*
Oxford University Printing House. . . .108
Pearl, type size. *119*
Pica, type size. *119*
Pont sizes. *119*
Printing bar. 107, *110*
Punchcutters. 103, 107, *108*
Punches, steel 103, 107, *108, 109*
Reid, Whitelaw. 103, 105, *112*, 116
Slugs, Linotype. *110*
Small pica, type size *119*
Specimen, Linotype type, 1888 116
"Strike," into copper bar. 107, *109*
Space band *110*
Spaces, hand type 114
Stereotyper .114
Thompson, G.L. 104
"Tribune Book of Open-Air Sports". .103, 116, *120, 121*
Type engravers 103, 107, *108*
Type casting mold. 107, *109*

PHOTOGRAPHIC ACKNOWLEDGEMENTS

Our thanks are extended to the following organizations and individuals who made illustration materials available to enhance the text of this book:

Page(s) 102: Corban Goble
  112: Library of Congress, Whitelaw Reid Papers
  ii, 96, 118: Linotype Company Archives, Steve Byers, Joe Mozzella
  112: Norman Cordes
  95: The New-York Historical Society
  xvii, 98: The New York Public Library, General Research Division, Astor, Lenox and Tilden Foundations
  108: Printer to the University of Oxford, Oxford, England

An editorial from Editor & Publisher magazine of May 1, 1920–

The Genius of the Workshop

The American Newspaper Publishers Association has unanimously voted to present the name of Ottmar Mergenthaler, Linotype inventor, as a candidate for the Hall of Fame [of Great Americans].

Had this man been a statesman, a rich banker or a great prince of commerce there would have been nothing to excite remark in the honor proposed for him. But the world is growing better. Men are learning to distinguish sometimes between the highly polished gilding and the raw true gold.

To the plain mechanic is due perhaps more than to any other man the marvelous development of typesetting machinery in the world's enlightenment and work. Through his genius the spread of knowledge and the activity of all business has been immeasurably extended and quickened. He is as true a benefactor of mankind as is known to our generation.

To the man who furnishes the capital, builds the factory and directs the sale of the product, richly lining his own pocket, the world has long been accustomed to pay reverence. It is a good thing, for a change, to take off our hats to the man who furnishes the ideas–whose brain and brawn, passing through the crucible, turn to gold. It will be a charming relief to exalt one of the few men who have really enriched the world by giving it a new idea.

Customs and public opinion move in cycles. In this nomination of a mechanic for the Hall of Fame, there is suggestion of the same spirit that marked the wisdom of Solomon at the great feast in honor of completion of the Temple, when the fine artists in mosaics, the skilled cutters of stone, the expert workers in wood and precious metals were all waved aside by the great king, and the humble, hard-handed blacksmith, Tubal Cain, was given the high seat of honor, because he had made the tools with which all these others had worked their wonders.

―――――

(Comment from the Springfield Daily Republican, May 5, 1920):

Whether or not Ottmar Mergenthaler, who has been nominated for the Hall of Fame, is elected, there will be very few printed notes regarding the election that will not have been produced with the aid of his genius.

―――

Mr. Mergenthaler was not elected.

⟨ COLOPHON ⟩

This book has done a bit of traveling before reaching the reader. The editor created and designed it in Rutherford, New Jersey. Typesetting of front matter and Part III was done at JCH Graphics in New York City, using a Linotronic 300 laser imagesetter. The typeface selected was Linotype Centennial, created by Adrian Frutiger especially for the Linotype Company's 100th anniversary in 1986. Some type was also set by True Type Printing Company in New York, and Part II was image-set by Pioneer Press in Terra Alta, West Virginia. Pioneer Press also did all the platemaking and presswork. Bookbinding took place at John A. Dekker & Son in Grand Rapids, Michigan, from where it was shipped to the publisher in New Castle, Delaware. The book is printed on 80-lb. Mohawk Vellum acid-free paper, which has a 300-year storage life.

May this book bring you new knowledge.